PROVERBS

God's Book of Wisdom

KJV (Simplified)

BY

Dr. Gerry D. Fox

The biblical references are my own iterations of scriptures from the King James Version that I have simplified to replace Old English with current English grammar and punctuation for quick, understandable reading.

CONTENTS

AUTHOR'S STORY

I had a pretty tough childhood, struggling with who I was and where I fit in. I was shy, and I think when a kid is shy, they end up being misunderstood. My shyness created a lot of insecurities which lead to a tiring battle of identity.

I have an older sister who loves me and thought it was her job to raise me. One day when I was sixteen, she said, "You need to read the Bible!"

I told her, "I wouldn't know what to read, and if I did, I wouldn't understand it."

She said, "Look, the book of Proverbs is God's book of wisdom. There are thirty-one chapters, one for each day of the month. If you don't know what to read and it's the fourteenth day of the month, read the fourteenth one."

I thought, "I can at least do that." I accepted her challenge, and very soon I was loving what I read. It changed my life forever.

This piece of advice helped me so much that I eventually became interested in other books of the Bible. I always came back to the basic idea she suggested. If I didn't know what to read and it was the fourteenth, the twenty-first, or the seventh day of the month, I'd pick it up and read that corresponding day in Proverbs. It was a brilliant, simple, and life-changing concept given to me by someone who loved me.

You may find this hard to believe, but I love you because God has given me the ability to feel great love for all His children through my journey with Him. I want you to experience the positive, uplifting, life-changing experiences I have had as I've continued to follow my sister's advice.

I have continued to read Proverbs almost daily. When I was twenty-one, my father gave me a little booklet titled *Living Proverbs* that I carried with me everywhere I went, and it became a guidebook for my life. Back in the 1970s and '80s, we didn't have smartphones to read all the time, so having this little booklet with me everywhere was comforting. Whenever I needed something to occupy my mind, I read it over and over and over when I was bored, during lunches, or later while traveling. This little booklet was The Living Bible translation of Proverbs. After having read the King James version for five years, I would occasionally came across verses and think, "I'm not sure that's what the King James version means." What I was reading was so powerful, so good, and even so simple to follow that I would skip over the verses I thought needed clarifying and continue to read, thinking the same thing every time I came back across those particular verses, and I always thought I needed to fix it someday.

Fast-forward to age thirty. I was in my own private healthcare practice and still reading the *Living Proverbs* booklet over and over. I loved how Proverbs gave me confidence, understanding, and discernment and how it spoke to me about business ideas, wealth building, family, relationships, how to interact with others, and, most importantly, how to honor and trust God with every aspect of my life.

These wonderful benefits only scratch the surface of what you gain when you read this powerful book. Proverbs 3:5–6 states, "Trust in the Lord with all your heart and do not lean on your own understanding. In all your ways acknowledge Him and He shall direct your paths." It is so comforting to know that in any situation, an all-powerful, all-knowing, omnipotent God tells us if we simply trust in Him with all our heart, He will guide us.

If you want to experience this, try it now with whatever you're going through. Close your eyes and do as the verse tells you. See and feel yourself trusting the Lord with all your heart, not leaning on your own understanding, and feel the peace of God wash over you as you trust Him with all your heart. It doesn't matter what the situation is or how difficult things seem. This truly works. This is a promise from God, and if God promises us something, He is obligated to do what He says.

As my healthcare practice continued to grow, I decided to call the publisher of my little book of Proverbs and buy a case of a hundred booklets. It was the first case of several I would buy to give out to all of my patients or anyone I came across and felt led to give a copy.

I wanted to help people I cared about and loved as much as I had been helped. One day I called to order another hundred booklets, and the woman who answered the phone told me the booklet was no longer being printed. I felt a huge void in my heart, and at the same time, that still, small voice that occasionally speaks to us, told me I needed to create a little booklet of my own to hand out.

I attempted it once in 2001 after the terrorist attack on the World Trade Center buildings, but I had edited it so many times over a period of a couple of years that I didn't know the difference between what was the Bible and what were my own thoughts. Rather than making Proverbs easy to read and easy to understand, I found myself trying to explain every verse, which became very complex and complicated. I finally grew so weary of trying to accomplish what should have been a simple task that I finally just printed what I had, and it never turned out the way I wanted it. It was my own fault because I got so far off track.

It was the fall of 2021 when I felt the yearning again to give away the little booklet that had shaped my life so much, but this time I just wanted to create a booklet that replaced Old English words, grammar, and punctuation with current English words, grammar, and punctuation. It had to be small enough to carry in a pocket or handbag and be at a price point where I could give away many copies. I worked on this project for about a year, and in the fall of 2022, *The Book of Proverbs: God's Book of Wisdom* was finally in print and not only in a small, pocket-sized booklet. A hardback book, an eBook, and audiobook were also created and available. The booklet turned out exactly the way I had envisioned it. Much to my surprise, without any advertising but definitely by the grace of God, people were buying this book in seven countries on four continents.

To date, I have now given away over 800 copies to people everywhere I go.

Life then threw me some curve balls, and I went through some major health and personal challenges for several years. These challenges began to peak to a point of hopelessness and even depression. But the book of Proverbs again came to my rescue.

Out of the blue, I thought about my friend Mark Victor Hansen. I met Mark back in the early 1990s through his motivational speaking at many seminars I attended. I loved listening to him, so I bought all of his motivational cassette tapes and listened to them over and over. Back then, he invited me to a special concentrated seminar he was putting on in Orange County, California, titled "Moneymaking in the '90s." I went to this four-day seminar that was held just prior to the launch of the first Chicken Soup for the Soul book and gained a wealth of knowledge.

During my struggles, I remembered all of Mark's motivational tapes and wanted to listen to them again. After moving several times, I no longer had them, so I started searching online for someone who might be wanting to sell theirs. I couldn't find any, but one day I stumbled across the Mark Victor Hansen Library publishing company, and there was my old friend's pictures on multiple books and audiobooks.

We hadn't seen each other in over thirty years, but I remembered that Mark is a voracious reader and loves to read everything he can get his hands on. With no ulterior motives, I decided to send him a couple of copies of my little Proverbs book, so I wrote him a letter and put them in the mail. I actually forgot I had sent them, and about a week or two later, my phone rang. The caller ID showed, "Mark Victor Hansen." This was quite a surprise! After we caught up for a few minutes, he told me how much he loved my book and the simplicity of there being thirty-one chapters, one for every day of the month. He said, "What a great idea! I have never thought of this. People need more wisdom, especially in today's world."

He then said, "This is not why I called, but I have a publishing company, and I would love to work with you to get this book out to more people."

We started talking daily, like best friends, with a common goal of getting *The Book of Proverbs* out to the masses. Mark truly is a marketing genius and shared lots of exciting ideas how we could get this life-changing book into the hands of many people. I hadn't told him this, but about a week before he called me, I had intently asked God if He would get this book into the hands of millions of people. Mark and I both agreed that God had brought us back together *for such a time as this*. We both want to help people gain wisdom and a closer walk with God all around the world.

I told Mark about my health challenges, and in his typical style, he said, "Working on this project will help heal you and make you feel better." You know, we started working on the updated version of this book, and it turns out he was absolutely correct. I feel like I have a whole new purpose, and I'm excited about the potential number of people this book can help.

I hope this book helps you as much as it has helped me, and, again, if you really want to see what this book will do, buy copies, give them out, and watch the transformations in those you love and care about. Give a copy to your pastor, family members, coworkers, or anyone, then sit back and watch. It is exciting and fulfilling to know you have helped others.

Many blessings!
Dr. Gerry D. Fox

FOREWORD

My friend, get ready for something truly life-changing! You are holding in your hands more than just a book. You are holding a daily appointment with **infinite wisdom**! This powerful little gem invites you to step into the timeless genius of the book of Proverbs one bite-sized miracle at a time. Read just one chapter a day every day of the month and watch your life soar to levels of success, peace, and mastery you never dreamed possible!

I know what this feels like because I've lived it. When I first encountered the profound simplicity of reading a proverb every single day, something extraordinary happened inside me. I was transformed! Wisdom isn't knowledge sitting on a shelf collecting dust. No! Wisdom is *actionable knowledge rightly applied*, the kind that delivers ever-better results on your thinking, your time, your energy, your money, and your very life. When you tap into real wisdom, you tap into your *greatest potential*!

Think about King Solomon for a moment. This incredible man went to God and asked for one thing: **wisdom**. Not riches. Not power. Not fame. Just wisdom! And because he asked for the right thing, God gave him everything else besides! Friend, Solomon's request is **your** request. It's *my* request. It's the fundamental cry of every heart that wants to live at the highest level. We were born to become competent, efficient, effective **masters of wisdom** in our field, profession, business, and life!

Author Dr. Gerry Fox, whom you're about to journey with, felt that same deep calling. He used the book of Proverbs as his personal GPS to guide him to greater success than he ever imagined possible, and now he's passionately sharing that same path with you. What a gift! He's distilled thirty-one life-changing proverbs—one for each day of the month—so you can cycle through them again and again, month after month, year after year, building a *natural storehouse of timeless wisdom* inside your heart and mind.

When you commit to this simple, powerful habit of reading *one proverb a day for the rest of your life,* something miraculous will unfold. You will align yourself with eternal truth and become more powerful, more successful, more peaceful, more *knowing.* Wisdom will guide your decisions, calm your storms, and light your way forward with unshakable confidence.

You deserve this! You were born for mastery, starting with mastering *yourself* through ever-increasing wisdom day by day, proverb by proverb, breakthrough by breakthrough!

So dive in! Read that first proverb today. Let it speak to you, let it change you, and then do it again tomorrow and the next day and the next. When you do, you'll **become** wise. You'll be stepping into the highest version of who you were created to be!

I believe in you with all my heart. The possibilities are endless. Your destiny is calling. Answer it one wise proverb at a time!

With infinite possibility and endless enthusiasm,

Mark Victor Hansen
Co-Creator of the *Chicken Soup for the Soul*® series, *Ask! The Bridge from Your Dreams to Your Destiny,* and *The One Minute Millionaire* series.

THE BOOK OF PROVERBS
GOD'S BOOK OF WISDOM

—

WISDOM'S CALL

Wisdom is contagious.

— Mark Victor Hansen

Stop what you're doing. Pause for a few moments and think. Can you imagine the Creator of Heaven and Earth taking His time to speak to you? That is an incredible thought in itself. Can you even begin to imagine how much wisdom, knowledge, and understanding can be gained by having wisdom itself speak to you? The thought of this is mind-boggling to me, but that is exactly what is happening here in this chapter as well as the entire Bible. Although Solomon's father, King David, was a powerful warrior, he must have had these same thoughts. Did you know he had a special prayer he would pray before reading God's word? He would pray, "Open my eyes, that I may see wondrous things from Your law" (Psalm 119:18).

King David's prayer is a very simple prayer, but if one of the most masculine men to ever walk the face of the earth felt it was important to hear from and have a relationship with God, don't you think we should want that as well? Prayer is us talking to God, and the Bible is God talking to us, so take this seriously and know that God would love to have a friendship with each of us. Before you read, ask God to speak to you through His word, and I promise you He will.

Now, pause a moment, take a breath, pray David's simple prayer, and as you read, sense the presence of God, the creator of Heaven and Earth.

1. The proverbs of Solomon, the son of David, King of Israel.

2. To know wisdom and instruction; to perceive the words of understanding.

3. To receive the instruction of wisdom, justice, judgment, and equity.

4. To give subtlety to the simple, to the young man knowledge and discretion.

5. A wise man will hear and increase learning, and a man of understanding shall listen to wise counsel.

6. To understand a proverb and the interpretation, the words of the wise and their dark sayings.

7. The fear of the LORD is the beginning of knowledge, but fools despise wisdom and instruction.

8. My son, hear the instruction of your father and forsake not the law of your mother;

9. For they shall be an ornament of grace to your head and chains on your neck.

10. My son, if sinners entice you, do not consent.

11. If they say, come with us, let us wait for blood, let us lurk privately for the innocent without cause;

12. Let us swallow them up alive as the grave, and whole, as those that go down into the pit.

13. We will find all precious substances; we shall fill our houses with spoil.

14. Cast in your lot among us; let us all have one purse.

15. My son, walk not in the way with them; refrain your foot from their path;

16. For their feet run to evil and make haste to shed blood.

17. Surely in vain the net is spread in the sight of any bird.

18. And they lie waiting for their own blood; they lurk privately for their own lives.

19. So are the ways of everyone that is greedy of gain, which takes away the life of the owners.

20. Wisdom cries out; she utters her voice in the streets;

21. She cries in the chief places of concourse, in the openings of the gates, in the city she utters her words, saying,

22. How long, you simple ones, will you love simplicity? And scorners delight in their scorning and fools hate knowledge?

23. Turn at my reproof; behold, I will pour out my spirit to you, and I will make my words known to you.

24. Because I have called and you refused, I have stretched out my hand and no one regarded.

25. But you have set at naught all my counsel and would have none of my reproof; therefore,

26. I will laugh at your calamity, and I will mock when your fear comes.

27. When your fear comes as desolation and your destruction comes as a whirlwind, when distress and anguish come upon you;

28. Then will you call upon me, but I will not answer. They shall seek me early, but they shall not find me.

29. For they hated knowledge and did not choose the fear of the LORD.

30. They would have none of my counsel, and they despised all my reproof.

31. Therefore, shall they eat of the fruit of their own way and be filled with their own devices.

32. For the turning away of the simple shall slay them, and the prosperity of fools shall destroy them.

33. But whoever hearkens unto me shall dwell safely and shall be quiet from fear of evil.

—

THE TREASURE OF WISDOM

An investment in knowledge
[wisdom] pays the best interest.

— Benjamin Franklin

There was a time in my life prior to age sixteen and before I was introduced to the book of Proverbs when I was hanging around with the wrong people and walking the wrong paths. They were paths of destruction. I'm sure most of us, at some point in our lives, have been on destructive paths and kept the wrong friends. I'm not proud of those days, but it taught me the pain of walking the wrong way with the wrong friends.

I am so thankful for the book of Proverbs and my sister, Pam, because what I learned, especially in this chapter, was profound and life-changing. Can you imagine a teenager being given a guidebook that helped them choose between right and wrong? This guidebook showed me in advance how my life could turn out if I chose the wrong way but how wonderful it could be if I chose the right way. One day when I was in my mid-thirties, loving life and receiving so many blessings from God, my younger brother, Marlon, and I were talking. Marlon asked me a profound question that shook me to the core and filled me with even more gratitude for the book of Proverbs. His question was, "Do you know how many of the friends, we grew up with are either in prison or dead from drug overdoses?" Thank you, Lord, for this book and my sister for giving me a simple way to read it!

1. My son, if you will receive my words and hide my commandments with you;

2. So that you incline your ear unto wisdom and apply your heart to understanding;

3. Yes, if you cry after knowledge and lift up your voice for understanding;

4. If you seek her as silver and search for her as for hidden treasures;

5. Then you shall understand the fear of the LORD and find the knowledge of God.

6. For the LORD gives wisdom; out of his mouth comes knowledge and understanding.

7. He lays up sound wisdom for the righteous; He is a buckler to them that walk uprightly.

8. He keeps the paths of judgment and preserves the way of his saints.

9. Then you will understand righteousness, judgment and equity; yes, every good path.

10. When wisdom enters into your heart, and knowledge is pleasant to your soul;

11. Discretion shall preserve you and understanding shall keep you;

12. To deliver you from the way of the evil man, from the man that speaks forward things;

13. Who leave the paths of uprightness, to walk in the ways of darkness;

14. Who rejoice to do evil and delight in the forwardness of the wicked;

15. Whose ways are crooked, and they froward in their paths;

16. To deliver you from the strange woman, even from the stranger who flatters with her words;

17. Who forsakes the guide of her youth and forgets the covenant of her God.

18. For her house inclines unto death and her paths unto the dead.

19. None that go into her return, neither will they take hold of the paths of life.

20. That you may walk in the way of good men and keep the paths of the righteous.

21. For the upright shall dwell in the land, and the perfect shall remain in it.

22. But the wicked shall be cut off from the earth, and
the transgressors shall be rooted out of it.

PROBERBS 3

—

TRUST & GUIDANCE

*Never be afraid to trust an unknown future
to a known God.*

— Corrie ten Boom

I was completely blown away the very first time I read this chapter to think of wisdom being more valuable than silver, gold, and rubies and that with wisdom would come riches, honor, and the Lord's guaranteed safety. This book had my attention! Why would I not want to follow it?

Reading wasn't one of my favorite things to do, but the simplicity of there being thirty-one chapters, one for each day of the month, was doable and positively changed my life forever. I had had my fill of choosing the wrong paths, and this was a simple challenge. All I had to do was seek wisdom with all my heart, and it would result in many blessings, but the opposite would be true if I chose not to. It wasn't always easy to stay on track, but I've always believed that anything worth having is not always easy to acquire. I loved this newly found guidebook for life.

Looking back, I can now see the amazing blessings I have gained in my life from my extraordinary God-given wife, three of the most incredible children, and ten of the sweetest grandchildren a person could ever want, including financial blessings as well. I know I sound like a proud husband, father, and grandfather, and I am, but I honestly shudder to think how my life would have turned out if I hadn't made a decision to follow my sister, Pam's, simple advice, continually reading the book of Proverbs, my guide book for life, over and over and over. And it's almost magical that no matter how many times I read and reread the book of Proverbs, or anything in the Bible for that matter, it seems like I always learn something new.

All of that being said, one of the greatest benefits I came to realize from reading Proverbs, is that it created a segue for me to eventually start reading the other books of the Bible, God's "expanded" guide book for life!

1. My son, forget not my law, but let your heart keep my commandments;

2. For length of days, long life, and peace shall they add to you.

3. Let not mercy and truth forsake you; bind them around your neck and write them upon the table of your heart:

4. So shall you find favor and good understanding in the sight of God and man.

5. Trust in the LORD with all your heart and lean not unto your own understanding.

6. In all your ways acknowledge Him, and He will direct your paths.

7. Be not wise in your own eyes; fear the LORD and depart from evil.

8. It shall be health to your navel and marrow to your bones.

9. Honor the LORD your substance and with the first fruits of all your increase:

10. So shall your barns be filled with plenty and your presses shall burst out with new wine.

11. My son, do not despise the chastening of the LORD; neither be weary of his correction;

12. For whom the LORD loves He corrects; even as a father the son in whom he delights.

13. Happy is the man that finds wisdom, and the man that gets understanding.

14. For the merchandise of it is better than the merchandise of silver and the gain than that of fine gold.

15. She is more precious than rubies, and all the things you can desire are not to be compared unto her.

16. Length of days is in her right hand, and in her left hand are riches and honor.

17. Her ways are ways of pleasantness, and all her paths are peace.

18. She is a tree of life to them that take hold of her, and happy is everyone who retains her.

19. The LORD by wisdom founded the earth; by understanding He established the heavens,

20. By His knowledge the depths are broken up and the clouds drop down the dew.

21. My son, don't let them depart from your eyes. Keep sound wisdom and discretion.

22. So shall they be life to your soul and grace to your neck.

23. Then shall you walk in your way safely, and your foot shall not stumble.

24. When you lie down, you shall not be afraid; yes, you shall lie down and your sleep shall be sweet.

25. Be not afraid of sudden fear, neither of the desolation of the wicked, when it comes.

26. For the LORD shall be your confidence and shall keep your foot from being taken.

27. Withhold not good from them to whom it is due, when it is in the power of your hand to do it.

28. Say not to your neighbor, "Go, and come again, and tomorrow I will give," when you have it by you.

29. Do not devise evil against your neighbor, seeing he dwells securely by you.

30. Strive not with a man without cause, if he has done you no harm.

31. Do not envy the oppressor and choose none of his ways;

32. For the froward is an abomination to the LORD: but His secret is with the righteous.

33. The curse of the LORD is in the house of the wicked, but He blesses the habitation of the just.

34. Surely, He scorns the scorners, but He gives grace unto the lowly.

35. The wise shall inherit glory, but shame shall be the promotion of fools.

GUARD YOUR HEART

*Life can only be understood backwards; but it must be
lived forwards. We must come back from the future in
our container of visualizations.*

— Søren Kierkegaard

High school was a very difficult time for me. The area
where I grew up probably wasn't much different than
today in that we all have choices to make regarding the
types of people we hang around. It is our own choice, but
sometimes those choices aren't as easy as you would think.
I remember one time when I was a junior or senior and it
was time for the junior-senior prom. On the weekend of the
prom, a lot of the students would share the cost of different beach houses with their closest friends, and, of course,
it was a big party weekend including lots of drinking and
what my dad would call carousing.

A couple of years before this prom, I was fifteen and had
decided that I wanted to change and do something valuable with my life. It started one day in a class where we

were allowed to talk, and the girl behind me asked me how many kids I wanted. I mean, come on! I was fifteen years old. How many kids do I want? Well, that did get me thinking. I looked at her and said, "Two or three."

Then she asked, "Boys or girls?"

I thought for a minute and said, "Well, actually, I think I'd like to have a boy, a girl, and the third one could be a boy or a girl. I guess I'd like to have a boy first, so he could protect his younger brother or sister."

You know, it's amazing how things turn out. We have three grown children and now ten grandchildren. Our children are all in their thirties now. The oldest is a boy named Michael, then we have Emily and Amy, so those dreams came true. Each of our kids have incredible character, impeccable integrity and are the most amazing people I've ever known. That question from the girl in my class, Renee, really put me on the spot, but it made me think that I needed to prepare myself to be able to take care of a wife and two or three children. That was a wake-up call! Thank you so much, Renee and God, who put that question in her mind to ask me!

* * *

That brief conversation was a wake-up call at age fifteen that prepared me for the book of Proverbs, my guidebook, that I would be given in the very near future.

Let me get back to why that's all important. It seemed I was now living in a period of time where I was between paths of right and wrong. The messages in the book of Proverbs were very clear messages from God to me. We have to remember that prayer is us talking to God and the Bible is God talking to us. It was like I could sense Him speaking to me as I focused on the words I read.

This particular prom weekend, I had learned that I had to keep myself focused on studying, but I still wanted to go to the beach for junior-senior weekend. That, of course, would be a joke because I didn't drink, I didn't smoke, and I didn't carouse anymore. I was staying focused on a better path for my life.

One day a couple of weeks before this particular weekend, I just had a strong urge that I wanted to go to the beach, but, of course, I didn't have funds to rent a beach house by myself. I did have friends, but again, beach houses were expensive to rent. I remember looking up to Heaven and saying, "God, I know it's impossible for me to go stay at the beach, but I sure would like to." I was, however, content with the state that I was in and okay if it didn't work out. But something amazing happened!

To this day, I still believe it was an angel, but a girl in our school came up to me between classes and said, "I'm supposed to give you these." She then handed me a set of keys. When I asked what it was, she said, "I own a house at the beach, and I'm supposed to let you stay there junior-senior weekend." I was really confused because I thought she was a student, but why would she have her own house? I had not told anyone about my brief prayer, and yet God answered with a blessing that only He and I knew about.

I truly believe God was blessing me because I had chosen to walk a righteous path rather than the destructive paths I had been on. This is just one example of the many, many blessings God has poured upon me. I believe it has to do with choosing the right paths. Now, I'm not saying that I've always done everything right. That would be impossible, but like 1 John 1:9 says, "If we confess our sins, He is faithful and just to forgive us our sins and to cleanse us from all unrighteousness."

I strongly encourage you to choose the right paths because God says the desires of our heart are from Him. He wants to bless us, but we must look to Him. Reading Proverbs, God's book of wisdom, is the easiest way to get started.

1. Hear, you children, the instruction of a father and attend to know understanding,

2. For I give you good doctrine; forsake not my law.

3. For I was my father's son, tender and only beloved in the sight of my mother.

4. He taught me and said, let your heart retain my words, keep my commandments and live.

5. Get wisdom, get understanding, and do not forget it; do not decline from the words of my mouth.

6. Forsake her not, and she will preserve you; love her and she will keep you.

7. Wisdom is the principal thing; therefore, get wisdom, and with all your getting, get understanding.

8. Exalt her, and she shall promote you; she shall bring you to honor when you embrace her.

9. She shall give to your head an ornament of grace, and a crown of glory shall she deliver to you.

10. Hear, O my son, and receive my sayings; and the years of your life shall be many.

11. I have taught you in the way of wisdom; I have led you in the right paths.

12. When you go, your steps shall not be straightened; and when you run, you shall not stumble.

13. Take fast hold of instruction, let her not go and keep her; for she is your life.

14. Enter not into the path of the wicked and go not in the way of evil men.

15. Avoid it, pass not by it, turn from it, and pass away.

16. For they sleep not, except they have done mischief; and their sleep is taken away, unless they cause some to fall.

17. For they eat the bread of wickedness and drink the wine of violence.

18. But the path of the just is as the shining light, that shines more and more unto the perfect day.

19. The way of the wicked is as darkness; they know not at what they stumble.

20. My son, attend to my words; incline your ear unto my sayings.

21. Let them not depart from your eyes; keep them in the midst of your heart.

22. For they are life to those who find them and health to all their flesh.

23. Keep your heart with all diligence, for out of it are the issues of life.

24. Put away from you a froward mouth, and perverse lips put far from you.

25. Let your eyes look right on, and let your eyelids look straight before you.

26. Ponder the path of your feet, and let all your ways be established.

27. Turn not to the right hand nor to the left, and remove your foot from evil.

PROVERBS 5

—

THE PATH OF
FAITHFULNESS

Do all the good you can… as long
as ever you can.

— John Wesley

When I was a young man and just starting to read Proverbs, my dad told me to read this chapter first and pay attention because these choices would literally mold the rest of my life. This is a very difficult chapter to consider and think about.

Dad indicated this would result in either lifelong bad consequences or unimaginable abundant blessings. I don't know about you, but I always wanted abundant blessings in my life.

The great thing about choosing to *be a child of God* is that He forgives all sins and shortcomings. This includes breaking any of the ten commandments, and we can start fresh again, knowing that if we confess and repent of any sin, God remembers it no more.

I encourage all young women and men to pay close attention to this chapter. It's a profoundly simple decision to always do the right thing, and it is so worth it. Like I've heard my wonderful wife, Belinda, say so many times, "Do right till the stars fall."

1. My son, attend unto my wisdom and bow your ear to my understanding:

2. That you may regard discretion, and your lips may keep knowledge.

3. For the lips of a strange woman drop as a honeycomb, and her mouth is smoother than oil;

4. But her end is bitter as wormwood, sharp as a two-edged sword.

5. Her feet go down to death; her steps take hold on hell.

6. Lest you should ponder the path of life, her ways are moveable, that you cannot know them.

7. Hear me now, therefore, O ye children, and depart not from the words of my mouth.

8. Remove your way far from her and come not near the door of her house;

9. Lest you give your honor unto others and your years unto the cruel;

10. Lest strangers be filled with your wealth and your labors be in the house of a stranger;

11. And you mourn at the last, when your flesh and
    your body are consumed,

12. And say, how have I hated instruction and my
    heart despised reproof;

13. And have not obeyed the voice of my teachers, nor
    inclined my ear to them that instructed me!

14. I was almost in all evil in the midst of the
    congregation and assembly.

15. Drink water out of your own cistern and running
    water out of your own well.

16. Let your fountains be dispersed abroad and rivers
    of water in the streets.

17. Let them be only your own and not for strangers
    with you.

18. Let your fountain be blessed and rejoice with the
    wife of your youth.

19. Let her be as the loving hind and pleasant roe,
    let her breasts always satisfy you and always be
    ravished with her love.

20. And why will you, my son, be ravished with
    a strange woman and embrace the bosom of a
    stranger?

21. For the ways of man are before the eyes of the
    LORD, and He ponders all his goings.

22. His own iniquities shall take the wicked himself,
    and he shall be held with the cords of his sins.

23. He shall die without instruction, and in the great-
    ness of his folly he shall go astray.

—

DILIGENCE VS. SLOTHFULNESS

Discipline is the bridge between goals and
accomplishment.

— Jim Rohn

Many times in life, we come across situations that test our integrity and character. If you're like me, the memory of some of the deep teachings from our parents, even grandparents, and possibly teachers will come to memory at just the right time.

This may be a time when we're making a decision that will have lifelong results. Trust me, they will come. God chose our parents to be the parents He felt best for us. I'm not saying that our parents are perfect. We are all human. But for some reason, God believes they are the best parents for us. I know as a teenager, I didn't think my parents knew anything and that I was smarter than them. Looking back over my life, I realized the things they were teaching me was for my own good, as painful as it may have felt at the time. Don't get me wrong. I had wonderful parents, and the more I accepted and learned to believe God had a purpose for putting me where he did, the better things got and the more wonderful things I learned. As the common saying goes, "The older I got, the smarter my parents became."

Look at the ants that are endlessly hard-working with organized diligence in Solomon's example. Dad told me they work in the summer preparing for winter and work in the winter preparing for summer. The ants exemplify wisdom by relentlessly improving their lives and surroundings. Stop, take a deep breath, smile, and repeat the prayer mentioned above from King David.

1. My son, if you are surety for your friend, if you have shaken your hand with a stranger,

2. You are snared with the words of your mouth; you are taken with the words of your mouth.

3. Do this now, my son, and deliver yourself, when you come into the hand of your friend; go, humble yourself and make sure your friend.

4. Give not sleep to your eyes, nor slumber to your eyelids.

5. Deliver yourself as a roe from the hand of the hunter and as a bird from the hand of the fowler.

6. Go to the ant, you sluggard; consider her ways and be wise;

7. Which having no guide, overseer or ruler,

8. Provides her meat in the summer and gathers her food in the harvest.

9. How long will you sleep, O sluggard? When will you arise out of your sleep?

10. A little sleep, a little slumber, a little folding of the hands to sleep;

11. So shall your poverty come as one that travels and your want as an armed man.

12. A naughty person, a wicked man, walks with a froward mouth.

13. He winks with his eyes, he speaks with his feet, and he teaches with his fingers.

14. Forwardness is in his heart; he devises mischief continually; he spreads discord.

15. Therefore shall his calamity come suddenly; suddenly shall he be broken without remedy.

16. These six things do the LORD hate: yes, seven are an abomination unto him:

17. A proud look, a lying tongue, and hands that shed innocent blood,

18. A heart that devises wicked imaginations, feet that are swift in running to mischief,

19. A false witness that speaks lies and spreads discord among brethren.

20. My son, keep your father's commandment and forsake not the law of your mother.

21. Bind them continually upon your heart and tie them around your neck.

22. When you go, it will lead you; when you sleep, it will keep you; and when you awaken, it will talk with you.

23. For the commandment is a lamp, the law is light, and reproofs of instruction are the way of life;

24. To keep you from the evil woman, from the flattery of the tongue of a strange woman.

25. Lust not after her beauty in your heart, neither let her take you with her eyelids;

26. For by means of a whorish woman a man is brought to a piece of bread, and the adulteress will hunt for the precious life.

27. Can a man take fire in his bosom and his clothes not be burned?

28. Can one walk upon hot coals and his feet not be burned?

29. So is he who goes into his neighbor's wife; whosoever touches her shall not be innocent.

30. Men do not despise a thief, if he steals to satisfy his soul when he is hungry.

31. But if he is found, he will restore sevenfold; he will give all the substance of his house.

32. Whoever commits adultery lacks understanding and destroys his own soul.

33. A wound and dishonor shall he get, and his reproach shall not be wiped away;

34. For jealousy is the rage of a man, and he will not spare in the day of vengeance.

35. He will not regard any ransom, nor will he rest content, though you give many gifts.

—

KEEP TO WISDOM, FLEE FOLLY

Everything rises and falls on leadership.

— John Maxwell

Have you ever seen someone setting up a little trap to catch birds? I assume they're doing this for food, but the trap is usually very simple and has a board over a hole with a pivot point in the middle of the board. They usually sprinkle a little bird food around the trap and then they sprinkle a little on the top of the board. Whenever a bird steps on it, it quickly falls right into the trap so quickly the other birds don't catch on and do the same thing.

Now, what does this have to do with the book of Proverbs? A lot, actually. You see, this is especially relevant for the young women and men on whom this chapter focuses. I assure you, there will be times when a trap will be set for you, and the bait will be very appealing, very attractive, dressed sexy, speaking softly and seductively, and maybe even smelling good. We are being warned about the dangers of seductive women and men. They have nothing to lose and everything to gain—at your expense.

The problem, as this chapter warns, is that if we make a foolish decision, the devastating destruction is not even realized until it's too late. Just like the birds in my illustration, they didn't know that the trap was for their life.

Hebrews 11:25 states, "The pleasures of sin are only for a season." There will *always* be a price to pay for making the wrong decision. Choose wisely!

1. My son, keep my words and hold my commandments with you.

2. Keep my commandments and live. Keep my law as the apple of your eye.

3. Bind them upon your fingers and write them upon the table of your heart.

4. Say unto wisdom, you are my sister and call understanding your kinswoman;

5. That they may keep you from the strange woman, from the stranger who flatters with her words.

6. For at the window of my house, I looked through my casement,

7. And beheld among the simple ones, I discerned among the youths, a young man lacking understanding,

8. Passing through the street near her corner, and he went the way to her house,

9. In the twilight, in the evening, in the black and dark night;

10. And, behold, there met him a woman dressed like a harlot, and she was subtle of heart.

11. (She is loud, stubborn, and her feet abide not in her house.

12. Now is she out in the streets and lies waiting at every corner.)

13. So she caught him, kissed him, and with an impudent face said unto him,

14. I have peace offerings with me. This day have I paid my vows.

15. Therefore, I came out to meet you, diligently to seek your face, and I have found you.

16. I have decked my bed with coverings of tapestry, with carved works and fine linen of Egypt.

17. I have perfumed my bed with myrrh, aloe, and cinnamon.

18. Come, let us take our fill of love until the morning. Let us solace ourselves with love.

19. For the goodman is not at home; he has gone on a long journey.

20. He has taken a bag of money with him and will come home on the appointed day.

21. With her much fair speech she caused him to yield, with the flattering of her lips she forced him.

22. He goes after her straightway, as an ox goes to the slaughter, or as a fool to the correction of the stocks;

23. Till a dart strikes through his liver; as a bird hastens to the snare and knows not that it is for his life.

24. Hearken unto me now, therefore, O you children, and attend to the words of my mouth.

25. Let not your heart decline to her ways nor go astray in her paths.

26. For she has cast down many wounded; yes, many strong men have been slain by her.

27. Her house is the way to hell, going down to the chambers of death.

—

WISDOM BEFORE ALL

*If I have seen further, it is by standing on
the shoulders of giants.*

— Isaac Newton

I read the most important, simplest, easiest, book of all, written by Solomon as he heard God's voice. I started reading Proverbs fifty-three years ago and still can't read it enough.

Proverbs is simple, applicable, and eye-opening to just what I need when I need it.

For that lifetime of guidance, I am so very grateful.

1. Does not wisdom cry and understanding put forth her voice?

2. She stands in the top of high places, in the places of the paths.

3. She cries at the gates, at the entry of the city, and at the coming in at the doors.

4. Unto you, O men, I call, and my voice is to the sons of man.

5. O you simple, understand wisdom, and you fools be of an understanding heart.

6. Hear, for I will speak of excellent things, and the opening of my lips speak right things.

7. For my mouth shall speak truth, and wickedness is an abomination to my lips.

8. All the words of my mouth are in righteousness; there is nothing froward or perverse in them.

9. They are all plain to him that understands and right to them that find knowledge.

10. Receive my instruction, and not silver, and knowledge rather than choice gold.

11. For wisdom is better than rubies, and all the things that may be desired are not to be compared to it.

12. I, wisdom, dwell with prudence and find out knowledge of witty inventions.

13. The fear of the LORD is to hate evil, pride, arrogance, and the evil way, and the froward mouth, do I hate.

14. Counsel and sound wisdom is mine. I am understanding, and I have strength.

15. By me kings reign and princes decree justice.

16. By me princes and nobles rule, even all the judges of the earth.

17. I love them that love me, and those that seek me early shall find me.

18. Riches and honor are with me; yes, durable riches and righteousness.

19. My fruit is better than gold, yes, than fine gold, and my revenue is better than choice silver.

20. I lead in the way of righteousness, amid the paths of judgment;

21. That I may cause those that love me to inherit substance, and I will fill their treasuries.

22. The LORD possessed me in the beginning of His way, before His works of old.

23. I was set up from everlasting, from the beginning, or ever the earth was.

24. When there were no depths, I was brought forth, when there were no fountains abounding with water.

25. Before the mountains were settled, before the hills, I was brought forth;

26. While yet He had not made the earth, nor the fields, nor the highest part of the dust of the world.

27. When He prepared the heavens and set a compass upon the face of the depth, I was there.

28. When He established the clouds above, when He strengthened the fountains of the deep,

29. When He gave to the sea His decree, that the
    waters should not pass His commandment, when
    He appointed the foundations of the earth;

30. Then I was by Him, as one brought up with Him;
    and I was daily His delight, rejoicing always before
    Him;

31. Rejoicing in the habitable part of His earth; and my
    delights were with the sons of men.

32. Now, therefore, listen to me, O ye children, for
    blessed are they that keep my ways.

33. Hear instruction, be wise, and refuse it not.

34. Blessed is the man that hears me, watching daily at
    my gates and waiting at the posts of my doors.

35. For whoever finds me finds life and shall obtain
    favor of the LORD.

36. But he who sins against me wrongs his own soul.
    All those who hate me love death.

PROVERBS 9

—

TWO INVITATIONS

The happiness of your life depends upon
the quality of your thoughts.

— Marcus Aurelius

How willing are you to accept correction, instructions, or teaching? When someone tries to help you or teach you something, do you resist, or do you pay attention and see what you can learn? As this chapter emphasizes, "Give instruction to a wise man, and he will be wiser yet; teach a just man, and he will increase in learning" (Proverbs 9:9).

Here again, Wisdom is speaking directly to the reader. How valuable is it that Wisdom itself would speak to us? We should feel compelled to pay attention.

Wisdom believes knowing the dangers of a glamorous woman is so vital to your survival that Proverbs contrasts the blessings of walking in wisdom with the dangers of falling into the trap of being seduced.

Carefully mark in your heart and mind what your decision will be when this test comes, and please understand, you will be tested.

1. Wisdom has built her house and has hewn out her seven pillars.

2. She has killed her beasts; she has mingled her wine; she has also furnished her table.

3. She has sent forth her maidens. She cries upon the highest places of the city;

4. Whoever is simple, let him turn in here. As for him who wants understanding, she says to him,

5. Come, eat of my bread and drink of the wine I have mingled.

6. Forsake the foolish and live. Go in the way of understanding.

7. He that reproves a scorner gets shame, and he that rebukes a wicked man gets a blot.

8. Reprove not a scorner, lest he hate you; rebuke a wise man and he will love you.

9. Give instruction to a wise man and he will be yet wiser; teach a just man and he will increase in learning.

10. The fear of the LORD is the beginning of wisdom, and the knowledge of the Holy One is understanding.

11. For by me your days shall be multiplied and the years of your life shall be increased.

12. If you are wise, you are wise for yourself; but if you scorn, you alone shall bear it.

13. A foolish woman is clamorous. She is simple and knows nothing.

14. For she sits at the door of her house, on a seat in the high places of the city,

15. Calling to those who go right on their way.

16. Whoever is simple, let him turn in here; and as for him who wants understanding, she says to him,

17. Stolen waters are sweet and bread eaten in secret is pleasant.

18. But he knows not that the dead are there and that her guests are in the depths of hell.

—

THE WISE VS. THE FOOLISH

If you want to lift yourself up,
lift up someone else.

— Booker T. Washington

L ife is about being so conscious and self-disciplined to right action that you evolve and lift yourself up. Jesus said, "And if I am lifted up from the earth, I will draw all men to me" (John 12:32). That is a universal truism, and you will be lifting up countless others with your life and wise example.

The foolish people open their mouths and remove all doubt that they are foolish. Whereas the wise man says wise things and everyone listens, learns, and takes action. Recently, Mark Victor Hansen advised a good friend that there was about to be a serious water shortage in California. He explained that there has been no snow for five years in the Colorado River headwaters, which means no water in the Colorado River Project (CRP), the main water source that serves California, so California will soon be dehydrated. The friend listened to this wisdom and took action, buying a reserve of water to take him through the impending drought.

What wisdom can you tune in to and share each day that might make someone's life better or avert a disaster? Wisdom says we need to use our words for good deeds in our own life and to bless others.

1. The proverbs of Solomon. A wise son makes a glad father, but a foolish son is the heaviness of his mother.

2. Treasures of wickedness profit nothing, but righteousness delivers from death.

3. The LORD will not suffer the soul of the righteous to famish but he casts away the substance of the wicked.

4. He becomes poor that deals with a slack hand, but the hand of the diligent makes rich.

5. He that gathers in summer is a wise son, but he that sleeps in harvest is a son that causes shame.

6. Blessings are upon the head of the just, but violence covers the mouth of the wicked.

7. The memory of the just is blessed, but the name of the wicked shall rot.

8. The wise in heart will receive commandments, but a chattering fool will fall.

9. He that walks uprightly walks surely, but he that perverts his ways shall be known.

10. He that winks with the eye causes sorrow, but a chattering fool will fall.

11. The mouth of a righteous man is a well of life, but violence covers the mouth of the wicked.

12. Hatred stirs up strife, but love covers all sins.

13. In the lips of him that has understanding, wisdom is found, but a rod is for the back of him that is void of understanding.

14. Wise men preserve knowledge, but the mouth of the foolish is near destruction.

15. The rich man's wealth is his strong city; the destruction of the poor is their poverty.

16. The labor of the righteous tends to life; the fruit of the wicked to sin.

17. He is in the way of life that keeps instruction, but he that refuses reproof errs.

18. He that hides hatred with lying lips, and he that utters a slander is a fool.

19. In the multitude of words there lacks not sin, but he that refrains his lips is wise.

20. The tongue of the just is as choice silver; the heart of the wicked is of little worth.

21. The lips of the righteous feed many, but fools die for lack of wisdom.

22. The blessing of the LORD makes rich, and he adds no sorrow with it.

23. It is like sport to a fool to do mischief, but a man of understanding has wisdom.

24. The fear of the wicked shall come upon him, but the desire of the righteous shall be granted.

25. As the whirlwind passes, so is the wicked no more; but the righteous is an everlasting foundation.

26. As vinegar to the teeth and smoke to the eyes, so is the sluggard to them that send him.

27. The fear of the LORD prolongs days, but the years of the wicked shall be shortened.

28. The hope of the righteous shall be gladness, but the expectation of the wicked shall perish.

29. The way of the LORD is strength to the upright, but destruction shall be to the workers of iniquity.

30. The righteous shall never be removed, and the wicked shall not inhabit the earth.

31. The mouth of the just brings forth wisdom, but the forward tongue shall be cut out.

32. The lips of the righteous know what is acceptable, but the mouth of the wicked speaks perverseness.

—

INTEGRITY & GENEROSITY

*Not all of us can do great things but we can
do small things with great love.*

— Mother Teresa

There have been times in my life when I desperately needed to know or hear someone tell me the difference between being a righteous (good) person or a wicked (bad) person. I'm imaging you've felt the same confusion at times. If we're being honest with ourselves, we know the difference between right and wrong. Occasionally, I needed to be reminded of the difference in consequences between those two choices. In all reality, we all know we want to be good and not bad. But there were those times I needed to have those differences reinforced by the Word of God. This chapter simply describes many of the results of our choices as we go down one of these two paths.

Our choices—good or bad—affect everyone around us. Dr. B.J. Palmer, the American Chiropractor who further developed the Chiropractic practices his father founded and made it an acceptable healing art, said, "We never know how far reaching something we may think, say, or do today will touch the lives of millions tomorrow." And you know what? He is correct.

1. A false balance is an abomination to the LORD, but a just weight is his delight.

2. When pride comes, then comes shame, but with the lowly is wisdom.

3. The integrity of the upright shall guide them, but the perverseness of transgressors shall destroy them.

4. Riches profit not in the day of wrath, but righteousness delivers from death.

5. The righteousness of the perfect shall direct his way, but the wicked shall fall by his own wickedness.

6. The righteousness of the upright shall deliver them, but transgressors shall be taken in their own iniquity.

7. When a wicked man dies, his expectation shall perish, and the hope of unjust men perishes.

8. The righteous are delivered out of trouble, and the wicked come in his stead.

9. A hypocrite with his mouth destroys his neighbor, but through knowledge shall the just be delivered.

10. When it goes well with the righteous, the city rejoices; and when the wicked perish, there is shouting.

11. By the blessing of the upright, the city is exalted, but it is overthrown by the mouth of the wicked.

12. He that is void of wisdom despises his neighbor, but a man of understanding holds his peace.

13. A talebearer reveals secrets, but he that has a faithful spirit conceals the matter.

14. Where there is no counsel, the people fall but in the multitude of counselors there is safety.

15. He that is surety for a stranger will smart for it, and he that hates suretyship is sure.

16. A gracious woman retains honor, and strong men retain riches.

17. The merciful man does good to his own soul, but he that is cruel troubles his own flesh.

18. The wicked work a deceitful work, but to him that spreads righteousness shall be a sure reward.

19. As righteousness tends to life so, he that pursues evil pursues it to his own death.

20. They that are of a perverse heart are an abomination to the LORD, but such as are upright in their way are his delight.

21. Though hand joins in hand, the wicked shall not be unpunished; but the seed of the righteous shall be delivered.

22. As a jewel of gold in a swine's snout, so is a fair woman who is without discretion.

23. The desire of the righteous is only good; but the expectation of the wicked is wrath.

24. There are those that scatter and yet increase and there are those that withhold more than is needed, but it leads to poverty.

25. The liberal soul shall be made fat, and he that waters shall be watered also himself.

26. He that withholds grain, the people shall curse him, but blessings shall be upon the head of him that sells it.

27. He that diligently seeks good procures favor, but he that seeks mischief, it shall come unto him.

28. He that trusts in his riches shall fall, but the righteous shall flourish as a branch.

29. He that troubles his own house shall inherit the wind, and the fool shall be servant to the wise of heart.

30. The fruit of the righteous is a tree of life, and he that wins souls is wise.

31. Behold, the righteous shall be recompensed in the earth, much more the wicked and the sinner.

PROVERBS 12

TRUTH & WORK

Where there is no vision, there is no hope.

— George Washington Carver

There was a point in my life when I was tired of my life having no compass at all. Our choices will affect everything in our present and future. King Solomon is said to have been the wisest, and I might add the wealthiest, man who ever lived. Who wouldn't want to listen to the wisest and wealthiest man who ever lived, the man who asked God first and foremost above all blessings to bless him with wisdom?

I know I want to pay close attention and hopefully learn some of his secrets of success. One thing that has always been important to me is to have success in every aspect of my life, whether it's a successful family, career, or even friendships. I know in my early years, I always wanted to be successful at everything I did, and this drove me to not only read but study Proverbs repeatedly to gain as much wisdom as possible.

Be inspired to make wise decisions to get the best results in your life.

1. Whoever loves instruction loves knowledge, but he that hates reproof is stupid.

2. A good man obtains favor of the LORD, but a man of wicked devices will He condemn.

3. A man shall not be established by wickedness, but the root of the righteous shall not be moved.

4. A virtuous woman is a crown to her husband, but she that makes ashamed is as rottenness in his bones.

5. The thoughts of the righteous are right, but the counsels of the wicked are deceit.

6. The words of the wicked are to lie in wait for blood, but the mouth of the upright shall deliver them.

7. The wicked are overthrown, and are not, but the house of the righteous shall stand.

8. A man shall be commended according to his wisdom, but he that is of a perverse heart shall be despised.

9. He that is despised, and has a servant, is better than he that honors himself and lacks bread.

10. A righteous man regards the life of his beast, but the tender mercies of the wicked are cruel.

11. He that tills his land shall be satisfied with bread, but he that follows vain persons is void of understanding.

12. The wicked desire the net of evil men, but the root of the righteous yields fruit.

13. The wicked is snared by the transgression of his lips, but the just shall come out of trouble.

14. A man shall be satisfied with good by the fruit of his mouth, and the recompence of a man's hands shall be rendered unto him.

15. The way of a fool is right in his own eyes, but he that hearkens unto counsel is wise.

16. A fool's wrath is presently known, but a prudent man covers shame.

17. He that speaks truth shows righteousness but a false witness, deceit.

18. There is he that speaks like the piercings of a sword, but the tongue of the wise is health.

19. The lip of truth shall be established forever, but a lying tongue is but for a moment.

20. Deceit is in the heart of them that imagine evil, but to the counselors of peace is joy.

21. There shall no evil happen to the just, but the wicked will be filled with mischief.

22. Lying lips are an abomination to the LORD, but they that deal truly are his delight.

23. A prudent man conceals knowledge, but the hearts of fools proclaim foolishness.

24. The hand of the diligent shall bear rule, but the slothful will be put to forced labor.

25. Heaviness in the heart of man makes it stoop, but a good word makes it glad.

26. The righteous is more excellent than his neighbor, but the way of the wicked seduces them.

27. The slothful man roasts not that which he took in hunting, but the substance of a diligent man is precious.

28. In the way of righteousness is life and, in their pathway, there is no death.

—

WISDOM IN COMPANIONSHIP & DISCIPLINE

*The main thing is to keep the main thing
the main thing.*

— Dr. Stephen R. Covey

Do you want to make wise or foolish decisions?

Ever since the very first time I opened the book of Proverbs and read from it, I continually noticed there were comparisons between wisdom and foolishness. I decided early on that, for the rest of my life, I wanted others to think of me as a wise man. That became my lifelong aspiration.

Jesus said, "The thief does not come except to steal and to kill and to destroy. I have come that they might have life, and that they might have it more abundantly" (John 10:10). I wanted the better things in life. I wanted this abundance Jesus talked about. I didn't desire all the things that came along with being foolish and making foolish decisions because that path ended in poverty, shame, and destruction. I had grown up in poverty and knew that I couldn't live that way anymore.

There had to be a better way, and the book of Proverbs opened my eyes to the possibilities of a simple decision to choose wisdom over foolishness. I know this may sound a little crazy to some, but I honestly didn't know there was a book so simple to read and understand that explained how to gain wisdom and avoid foolishness.

I would always ask God to speak to me through these words, as I mentioned in an earlier chapter, to open my eyes that I might obtain wonderful things from His Word. It didn't take long for me to realize as God clearly spoke to me through these words that I was gaining a wealth of wisdom, knowledge, and understanding.

Many times, I read more than one Proverb per day, which gave me peace and understanding. I found Proverbs was more valuable than gold or silver and nothing could be compared to it.

Lao Tzu said, "The journey of a thousand miles begins with a single step." It's like running a mile or walking a mile. You still get all the health benefits of going a mile but one just gets there faster. As a hungry man for wisdom and abundant blessings, I kept this new book of wisdom and knowledge with me at all times, so I could learn how to become wise. I'm still working on it today.

What is it that you want? Do you want wisdom, wealth, and abundant blessings, or do you want to continue down a path of foolishness, a path of lack, destruction, loneliness, emotional pain, and everything that goes along with foolish decisions?

Dr. John C. Maxwell had a powerful life-changing quote that goes like this, "Though no one can change their past my friend, anyone can start from here and have a brand new end."

So be wise now and forevermore.

1. A wise son hears his father's instruction, but a scorner hears not rebuke.

2. A man shall eat good by the fruit of his mouth but the souls of the transgressors shall eat violence.

3. He that keeps his mouth keeps his life, but he that opens wide his lips shall have destruction.

4. The soul of the sluggard desires and has nothing, but the soul of the diligent shall be made fat.

5. A righteous man hates lying, but a wicked man is loathsome and comes to shame.

6. Righteousness keeps him that is upright in the way, but wickedness overthrows the sinner.

7. There is he that makes himself rich yet has nothing, and there is he that makes himself poor yet has great riches.

8. The ransom of a man's life is his riches, but the poor hears not rebuke.

9. The light of the righteous rejoices, but the lamp of the wicked shall be put out.

10. Only by pride comes contention, but with the well advised is wisdom.

11. Wealth gained by vanity shall be diminished, but he that gathers by labor shall increase.

12. Hope deferred makes the heart sick, but when the desire comes it is a tree of life.

13. Whoever despises the word shall be destroyed, but he that fears the commandment shall be rewarded.

14. The law of the wise is a fountain of life, to depart from the snares of death.

15. Good understanding gives favor, but the way of transgressors is hard.

16. Every prudent man deals with knowledge, but a fool lays open his folly.

17. A wicked messenger falls into mischief, but a faithful ambassador is health.

18. Poverty and shame shall be to him that refuses instruction, but he that regards reproof shall be honored.

19. The desire accomplished is sweet to the soul, but it is an abomination to fools to depart from evil.

20. He that walks with wise men shall be wise, but a companion of fools shall be destroyed.

21. Evil pursues sinners, but to the righteous good shall be repaid.

22. A good man leaves an inheritance to his children's children, and the wealth of the sinner is laid up for the just.

23. Much food is in the tillage of the poor, but there is he that is destroyed for lack of judgment.

24. He that spares his rod hates his son, but he that loves him chastens him early.

25. The righteous eats to the satisfying of his soul, but the belly of the wicked shall want.

—

REVERENCE & PRUDENCE

There are eight forms of charity. The highest form of charity is when you help a man help himself.

— Maimonides

Wow! Where do I even begin to talk about how much this chapter has played a part in molding my life for the good. It seems like every verse in this chapter has something powerful to say. I can remember over the years writing down some of these verses and carrying them with me through the day so that I could look back at them and think back over them all day. I could list so many things from this chapter alone that will resonate within you and guide you to make your life more enjoyable and better. I know it did for me and still does today.

I truly hope, from the depths of my heart, that you get the same benefits out of this chapter as I have or better, and the only way for you to find that out is to turn the page and start reading. I wouldn't read this chapter fast or even skim over it. I would suggest that you take your time to think about some of the most impactful verses. I think you'll understand why Chapter 14 has so many positively impactful messages that you will remember for the rest of your life.

One thing that has always stood out in my mind, since the very first time I read this chapter, was Proverbs 14:4, which states, "Where there are no oxen, the manger is clean, but much increase comes by the strength of the ox." That one verse can apply to so many things in our lives.

I think the first time it really hit home with me was when we had three young children. Before I got married, I was a kind of a neatnik and liked everything in its place. Some people say I'm a perfectionist, but I don't think so. I just like things being done right. Anyway, we homeschooled our children, and when I would come home from the office, there might be toys everywhere, and I just had to learn to step over them. I came up with my own version of Proverbs 14:4: "Where there are no children, the house is clean, but much love and joy comes from their presence."

I saw toys everywhere, but my incredible wife, Belinda, would always help me understand the toys were there because they had a great day of learning and fun. She also told me how the best memories were her sitting on the couch with the youngest child sitting on her lap and the other two pressed closely to her sides as she read books to them every day. That, my friend, makes it all worthwhile.

That is just one verse out of this entire chapter. Can you imagine what else you're going to be able to find in this chapter that is so life-changing?

1. Every wise woman builds her house, but the foolish plucks it down with her hands.

2. He that walks in his uprightness fears the LORD, but he that is perverse in his ways despises Him.

3. In the mouth of the foolish is a rod of pride, but the lips of the wise shall preserve them.

4. Where no oxen are, the crib is clean, but much increase is by the strength of the ox.

5. A faithful witness will not lie, but a false witness will utter lies.

6. A scorner seeks wisdom and finds it not, but knowledge is easy to him that understands.

7. Go from the presence of a foolish man, when you perceive not in him the lips of knowledge.

8. The wisdom of the prudent is to understand his way, but the folly of fools is deceit.

9. Fools make a mock at sin, but among the righteous there is favor.

10. The heart knows its own bitterness and a stranger does not meddle with its joy.

11. The house of the wicked shall be overthrown, but the tabernacle of the upright shall flourish.

12. There is a way which seems right unto a man, but the end thereof, are the ways of death.

13. Even in laughter the heart is sorrowful, and the end of that mirth is heaviness.

14. The backslider in heart shall be filled with his own ways, and a good man shall be satisfied from himself.

15. The simple believe every word, but the prudent man looks well to his going.

16. A wise man fears and departs from evil, but the fool rages and is confident.

17. He that is soon angry deals foolishly, and a man of wicked devices is hated.

18. The simple inherit folly, but the prudent are crowned with knowledge.

19. The evil bow before the good, and the wicked bow at the gates of the righteous.

20. The poor are hated even by their own neighbors, but the rich have many friends.

21. He that despises his neighbor, sins, but he that has mercy on the poor is happy.

22. Do they not err that devise evil? But mercy and truth shall be to them that devise good.

23. In all labor there is profit, but the talk of the lips leads only to poverty.

24. The crown of the wise is their riches, but the foolishness of fools is folly.

25. A true witness delivers souls, but a deceitful witness speaks lies.

26. In the fear of the LORD is strong confidence, and His children shall have a place of refuge.

27. The fear of the LORD is a fountain of life, to depart from the snares of death.

28. In the multitude of people is a king's honor, but in the lack of people is the destruction of a prince.

29. He that is slow to wrath is of great understanding, but he that is hasty of spirit exalts folly.

30. A sound heart is the life of the flesh, but envy is the rottenness of the bones.

31. He that oppresses the poor reproaches his Maker, but he that honors Him has mercy on the poor.

32. The wicked is driven away in his wickedness, but the righteous has hope in his death.

33. Wisdom rests in the heart of him who has understanding, but that which is in the midst of fools is made known.

34. Righteousness exalts a nation, but sin is a reproach to any people.

35. The king's favor is toward a wise servant, but his wrath is against him that causes shame.

—

SOFT ANSWERS, WISE TONGUES

Raise your words, not voice. It is rain that grows flowers, not thunder.

— Rumi

Will you allow yourself to absorb and gain the depths of wisdom, knowledge, and understanding? Right now, as I write this, I am in the mountains sitting by a quiet, beautiful, bubbling creek. I can sense the presence of God, and it's almost as if He is speaking directly to me through the words on the page. I hope you will take some time and find your quiet place in nature that resonates with you. Take this book along. When you find a beautiful, quiet place, let your mind relax as you read and enter the deepest core of your being. You will sense a deep feeling of peace and freedom wash over you if you can allow yourself the time away from your life, business and the hustle and bustle of your everyday routines.

The overall general concept that King Solomon wants to convey in the next pages is that our words are powerful, whether they be positive or negative. Whether we speak or hear them, our words affect ourselves and those around us. Proverbs is telling us to be careful how or what we speak and what we hear or listen to because the effects can and will be deep and far-reaching. From this point forward, choose your words carefully, whether spoken in the quietude of your mind or uttered allowed.

1. A soft answer turns away wrath, but grievous words stir up anger.

2. The tongue of the wise uses knowledge aright, but the mouth of fools pours out foolishness.

3. The eyes of the LORD are in every place watching the evil and the good.

4. A wholesome tongue is a tree of life, but perverseness is a breach in the spirit.

5. A fool despises his father's instruction, but he that regards reproof is prudent.

6. In the house of the righteous is much treasure, but in the revenues of the wicked is trouble.

7. The lips of the wise disperse knowledge, but the heart of fools does not.

8. The sacrifice of the wicked is an abomination to the LORD, but the prayer of the upright is his delight.

9. The way of the wicked is an abomination unto the LORD, but He loves him that follows after righteousness.

10. Correction is grievous unto him that forsakes the way, and he that hates reproof shall die.

11. Hell and destruction are before the LORD, so how much more the hearts of the children of men?

12. A scorner loves not one that reproves him, neither will he go unto the wise.

13. A merry heart makes a cheerful countenance, but by sorrow of the heart the spirit is broken.

14. The heart of him that has understanding seeks knowledge, but the mouth of fools feeds on foolishness.

15. All the days of the afflicted are evil, but he that is of a merry heart has a continual feast.

16. Better is little with the fear of the LORD than great treasure and trouble therewith.

17. Better is a dinner of herbs, where love is, than a stalled ox with hatred.

18. A wrathful man stirs up strife, but he that is slow to anger appeases strife.

19. The way of the slothful man is as a hedge of thorns, but the way of the righteous is made plain.

20. A wise son makes a glad father, but a foolish man despises his mother.

21. Folly is joy to him that is destitute of wisdom, but a man of understanding walks uprightly.

22. Without counsel purposes are disappointed, but in the multitude of counselors they are established.

23. A man has joy by the answer of his mouth, and a word spoken in due season, how good it is!

24. The way of life is above to the wise, that he may depart from hell beneath.

25. The LORD will destroy the house of the proud, but he will establish the border of the widow.

26. The thoughts of the wicked are an abomination to the LORD, but the words of the pure are pleasant.

27. He that is greedy of gain troubles his own house, but he that hates gifts shall live.

28. The heart of the righteous studies how to answer, but the mouth of the wicked pours out evil things.

29. The LORD is far from the wicked, but He hears the prayer of the righteous.

30. The light of the eyes rejoices the heart, and a good report makes the bones fat.

31. The ear that hears the reproofs of life abides among the wise.

32. He that refuses instruction despises his own soul, but he that hears reproof gets understanding.

33. The fear of the LORD is the instruction of wisdom, and before honor is humility.

PLANS, PROVIDENCE, & PRIDE

Your attitude, not your aptitude,
will determine your altitude.

— Zig Ziglar

Have you ever found yourself uncomfortable in a crowd, and you didn't know what to say or how to act or react around groups of people, whether they be family, friends, or strangers? I know I have, and although there are many valuable statements that could be remembered and thought upon in this chapter, one verse stands out that has helped me through uncomfortable positions many times over my entire life. I'm so thankful for Proverbs 16:7, which states, "When a man's ways please the LORD, He makes even his enemies to be at peace with him." I mean, how free does that set you in uncomfortable situations?

I might be having a down day or even a good day but not know how to handle certain situations where others were present, and all I had to remember was, if my ways please the Lord, He makes even my enemies be at peace with me. How comforting it is to know and to have known that I can have peace with my enemies by making my ways please the Lord. Just imagine how incredible it will be with those who are family or friends.

1. The preparations of the heart belong to man, and the answer of the tongue is from the LORD.

2. All the ways of a man are clean in his own eyes, but the LORD weighs the spirits.

3. Commit your works unto the LORD, and your thoughts shall be established.

4. The LORD made all things for himself, yes, even the wicked for the day of evil.

5. Everyone that is proud in heart is an abomination to the LORD; though hand join in hand, he shall not go unpunished.

6. By mercy and truth iniquity is purged, and by the fear of the LORD, men depart from evil.

7. When a man's ways please the LORD, he makes even his enemies to be at peace with him.

8. Better is a little with righteousness than great revenues without right.

9. A man's heart devises his way, but the LORD directs his steps.

10. A divine sentence is in the lips of the king, and his mouth transgresses not in judgment.

11. A just weight and balance are the LORD'S; all the weights of the bag are His work.

12. It is an abomination to kings to commit wickedness for the throne is established by righteousness.

13. Righteous lips are the delight of kings, and they love him that speaks right.

14. The wrath of a king is as messengers of death, but a wise man will pacify it.

15. In the light of the king's countenance is life, and his favor is like a cloud of the latter rain.

16. How much better it is to get wisdom than gold, and to get understanding is to be chosen rather than silver!

17. The highway of the upright is to depart from evil; he that keeps his way preserves his soul.

18. Pride goes before destruction and a haughty spirit before a fall.

19. Better it is to be of a humble spirit with the lowly than to divide the spoil with the proud.

20. He that handles a matter wisely shall find good, and whoever trusts in the LORD is happy.

21. The wise in heart shall be called prudent, and the sweetness of the lips increases learning.

22. Understanding is a wellspring of life to him that has it, but the instruction of fools is folly.

23. The heart of the wise teaches his mouth and adds learning to his lips.

24. Pleasant words are like a honeycomb, sweet to the soul and health to the bones.

25. There is a way that seems right unto a man, but the end thereof, is the way of death.

26. He that labors, labors for himself, for his mouth craves it of him.

27. An ungodly man digs up evil, and in his lips there is a burning fire.

28. A perverse man sows strife, and a whisperer separates chief friends.

29. A violent man entices his neighbor and leads him into a way that is not good.

30. He shuts his eyes to devise froward things, and moving his lips he brings evil to pass.

31. The hoary head is a crown of glory if it is found in the way of righteousness.

32. He that is slow to anger is better than the mighty, and he that rules his own spirit than he that takes a city.

33. The lot is cast into the lap, but the whole disposing thereof is of the LORD.

—

PEACE, FRIENDSHIP, RESTRAINT

Better to remain silent and be thought a fool than to speak and remove all doubt.

— Abraham Lincoln

Have you ever had a hard time controlling your tongue? There are several powerful verses that still resonate within the fibers of my being when it comes to managing myself with the words I speak.

I alluded in an earlier chapter that I grew up in an area that was a bit rough. For a shy kid like I was, coming from of a life filled with wrong decisions, it was difficult to learn these lessons but so worth the challenge and change. As a teenager, when I decided I needed to change the direction I was going, I realized I needed all the help I could get to at least appear wise. There's an old saying that states, "To be, act as if," and the book of Proverbs contained nearly everything I needed to make those changes.

I still occasionally struggle to control my tongue, but I continue to ask God and others to forgive me and keep moving forward.

James Chapter 3 in the Bible is all about controlling the tongue. I strongly recommend you take a few minutes and read it along with Proverb 17 if you struggle in this area. It clearly helped me understand the power of words, whether they be good, bad, positive, or negative.

1. Better is a dry morsel with quietness than a house full of sacrifices with strife.

2. A wise servant shall have rule over a son that causes shame and shall have part of the inheritance among the brethren.

3. The fining pot is for silver and the furnace for gold, but the LORD tries the hearts.

4. A wicked doer gives heed to false lips, and a liar gives ear to a mischievous tongue.

5. Whoever mocks the poor reproaches his Maker, and he that is glad at calamities shall not go unpunished.

6. Children's children are the crown of old men, and the glory of children are their fathers.

7. Excellent speech becomes not a fool, much less do lying lips a prince.

8. A gift is a precious stone in the eyes of him who has it, and wherever it turns, it prospers.

9.   He that covers a transgression seeks love, but he
     that repeats a matter separates very friends.

10. A reproof enters more into a wise man than a hun-
     dred stripes into a fool.

11. An evil man seeks only rebellion; therefore, a cruel
     messenger shall be sent against him.

12. Let a bear robbed of her whelps meet a man rather
     than a fool in his folly.

13. Whoever rewards evil for good, evil shall not
     depart from his house.

14. The beginning of strife is like when one lets out water;
     therefore, leave off contention before it is meddled
     with.

15. He that justifies the wicked and he that condemns
     the just are both an abomination to the LORD.

16. Why is there a price in the hand of a fool to get
     wisdom, seeing he has no heart to it?

17. A friend loves at all times, and a brother is born for
     adversity.

18. A man void of understanding strikes hands and
     becomes surety in the presence of his friend.

19. He loves transgression that loves strife, and he that
     exalts his gate seeks destruction.

20. He that has a froward heart finds no good, and he
     that has a perverse tongue falls into mischief.

21. He that begets a fool does it to his sorrow, and the father of a fool has no joy.

22. A merry heart does good like a medicine, but a broken spirit dries the bones.

23. A wicked man takes a gift out of the bosom to pervert the ways of judgment.

24. Wisdom is before him that has understanding, but the eyes of a fool are on the ends of the earth.

25. A foolish son is a grief to his father and bitterness to her that bore him.

26. To punish the just is not good nor to strike princes for their equity.

27. He that has knowledge spares his words, and a man of understanding is of an excellent spirit.

28. Even a fool, when he holds his peace, is counted wise, and he that shuts his lips is esteemed a man of understanding.

—

WORDS & WISDOM

*Wise men speak because they have something to say;
fools because they have to say something.*

— Plato

I think King Solomon is reminding us how to understand the importance of our words. He teaches us how careful we need to be with them because they can affect the outcomes of people we meet, know, and care about.

We are not meant to be alone. I want to have lots of friends, even though sometimes I feel like relationships are a bit awkward. "A man who has friends must show himself friendly, and there is a friend who sticks closer than a brother" (Proverbs 18:24) led me to an important discovery. I've discovered the friend who sticks closer than a brother is God. It feels good to know that God is always available, a friend and a pal.

He said in Deuteronomy 31:6, "Be strong and of good courage. Do not fear or be afraid of them, for the LORD your God, it is He who goes with you. He will not fail you or forsake you." Jesus promised His disciples in Matthew 28:20, "And behold, I am with you always, even to the end of the world." It is so comforting to know that I *always* have a friend, Jesus, who sticks closer than a brother.

The incredible concepts in the wonderful book of Proverbs can create your turning point. It is jam-packed with more valuable information that will sustain you in unthinkable ways throughout your life. So take a few minutes to soak it up, contemplate it, and let it all sink in deeply.

1. Through desire a man, having separated himself, seeks and intermeddles with all wisdom.

2. A fool has no delight in understanding, but that his heart may discover itself.

3. When the wicked comes, then also comes contempt, and with dishonor, disgrace.

4. The words of a man's mouth are as deep waters and the wellspring of wisdom, as a flowing brook.

5. It is not good to accept the person of the wicked or to overthrow the righteous in judgment.

6. A fool's lips enter into contention, and his mouth calls for strokes.

7. A fool's mouth is his destruction, and his lips are the snare of his soul.

8. The words of a talebearer are like wounds, and they go down into the innermost parts of the belly.

9. He that is slothful in his work is brother to him that is a great waster.

10. The name of the LORD is a strong tower; the righteous run into it and are safe.

11. The rich man's wealth is his strong city and like a high wall in his own conceit.

12. Before destruction the heart of man is haughty, and before honor is humility.

13. He that answers a matter before he hears it, it is folly and shame unto him.

14. The spirit of a man will sustain his infirmity, but a wounded spirit who can bear?

15. The heart of the prudent gets knowledge, and the ear of the wise seeks knowledge.

16. A man's gift makes room for him and brings him before great men.

17. He that is first in his own cause seems just, but his neighbor comes and searches him.

18. The lot causes contentions to cease and parts between the mighty.

19. A brother offended is harder to be won than a strong city, and their contentions are like the bars of a castle.

20. A man's belly shall be satisfied with the fruit of his mouth, and with the increase of his lips shall he be filled.

21. Death and life are in the power of the tongue, and they that love it shall eat the fruit thereof.

22. Whoever finds a wife finds a good thing and obtains favor of the LORD.

23. The poor use entreaties, but the rich answer roughly.

24. A man that has friends must show himself friendly, and there is a friend that sticks closer than a brother.

PROVERBS 19

—

PATIENCE, INTEGRITY, PRUDENCE

By perseverance the snail reached the ark.

— Charles Spurgeon

As a teen, I wanted to change and improve. When a person doesn't have direction, they tend to be slothful, lazy, and unfocused. Looking back to my early teen years, when I started reading the book of Proverbs, it became my lifeline for survival in that crazy world. My dad occasionally implied that I was lazy, but he always followed it with, "Gerry, you can do anything you put your mind to." Our words are powerful, and those words from my father struck a chord in me. They still encourage me to this very day.

Proverbs 19:15 states, "Slothfulness casts into a deep sleep, and an idle soul shall suffer hunger." I had already experienced feelings of want, living in confusion, and lack of awareness, but I knew instantly when I read this verse that I never wanted to suffer hunger.

I'm not saying fear is a good thing. The Bible says 365 times not to fear. Sometimes, fear can protect us and motivate us to get moving. Late one afternoon, close to dusk, I was walking around our neighborhood when I glanced down and saw a baby copperhead snake stretched out across the sidewalk exactly where my next step would have landed. I can tell you, by shear instinct and fear, I jumped to avoid stepping on it. So fear is a survival response that God put in our original equipment.

Einstein is thought to have said, "If you always do what you've always done, you'll always get what you've always got." I desperately wanted to change and have an abundant life, so I stayed busy believing Proverbs 14:23: "In all labor there is profit, but the talk of the lips leads only to poverty." I am a giver by nature, and what I came to learn years later is those profits could also help others who were in need. One of the greatest feelings you'll ever have is being able to give to and help others. God states in verse 17, "He who has compassion on the poor lends to the LORD, and He will repay him what he has given." Wow! God promises us if we are generous and have pity on the poor, He will repay us, and when He repays, it is always over and above what we can ever imagine or dream possible. It's my prayer that this serves you greatly.

1.   Better is the poor that walks in his integrity than he that is perverse in his lips and is a fool.

2.   Also, it is not good that the soul be without knowledge, and he that hastens with his feet sins.

3. The foolishness of a man perverts his way, and his heart frets against the LORD.

4. Wealth makes many friends, but the poor are separated from their neighbors.

5. A false witness shall not go unpunished, and he that speaks lies shall not escape.

6. Many will entreat the favor of the prince, and every man is a friend to him that gives gifts.

7. All the brethren of the poor hate him; how much more do his friends go far from him? He pursues them with words, yet they ignore him.

8. He that gets wisdom loves his own soul. He that keeps understanding shall find good.

9. A false witness shall not go unpunished, and he that speaks lies shall perish.

10. Delight is not seemly for a fool, much less for a servant to have rule over princes.

11. The discretion of a man defers his anger, and it is his glory to pass over a transgression.

12. The king's wrath is as the roaring of a lion, but his favor is as dew upon the grass.

13. A foolish son is the calamity of his father, and the contentions of a wife are a continual dropping.

14. House and riches are the inheritance of fathers, and a prudent wife is from the LORD.

15. Slothfulness casts into a deep sleep, and an idle soul shall suffer hunger.

16. He that keeps the commandment keeps his own soul, but he that despises his ways shall die.

17. He that has pity on the poor lends to the LORD, and that which he has given will He pay him again.

18. Chasten your son while there is hope and let not your soul spare for his crying.

19. A man of great wrath shall suffer punishment, and if you deliver him, you must do it again.

20. Hear counsel and receive instruction that you may be wise in your latter end.

21. There are many devices in a man's heart; nevertheless, the counsel of the LORD shall stand.

22. The desire of a man is his kindness, and a poor man is better than a liar.

23. The fear of the LORD tends to life, and he that has it shall abide satisfied; he shall not be visited with evil.

24. A slothful man hides his hand in his bosom and will not so much as bring it to his mouth again.

25. Smite a scorner, and the simple will beware. Reprove one that has understanding, and he will understand knowledge.

26. He that wastes his father and chases away his mother is a son that causes shame and brings reproach.

27. Cease, my son, to hear the instruction that causes you to stray from the words of knowledge.

28. An ungodly witness scorns judgment, and the mouth of the wicked devours iniquity.

29. Judgments are prepared for scorners and stripes for the backs of fools.

—

HONESTY & SELF-CONTROL

No great thing is created suddenly.

— Epictetus

King Solomon said, "In all labor there is profit" (Proverbs 14:23). What that taught me was not to sit idly waiting for my life to change but to stay busy, active, and doing positive things. I discovered if I didn't know what to do, one of the greatest things I could do was to help other people. I realized as a teenager that my parents needed help around the house, so I got busy. Without asking, I would do yard work, which soon inspired me to clean the house, wash the dishes, and do the laundry. I even started grocery shopping for them, which turned out to be kind of fun, especially during the holidays. They loved having my help. I did anything I could to take pressure off with them. I'm sure at times they wondered if I was really their son.

The profits I gained from just helping my parents, who were so busy working to provide for our family, were far greater than money. I gained respect for myself and appreciation from my parents, and that led into other areas of helping others. It felt so good to just give, seeking nothing in return.

To gain respect from others, it works to be a giver. If I had been invited to someone's home for a meal, I found great pleasure in pitching in. Jesus said in Luke 6:38,"Give, and it shall be given to you. Good measure—pressed down, and shaken together, and running over."

I decided to become a doctor because it would allow me to help people as well as earn enough income to care for a family. Soon after I began practice, I learned a very valuable lesson. I don't mean anything derogatory or degrading about this, but I went home to visit my parents driving a new Lincoln Town Car. I decided to drive by one of the hangout places we frequented as kids and say hi to some of my old friends. I thought I'd be welcomed back after having achieved some success, but quite the contrary happened. I pulled up to a place where some of the gang was hanging out. It was the same group of guys sitting on the same stumps, smoking the same brand of cigarettes. When I stopped, they all stood up and walked around my new car. I thought they were admiring it and maybe they were, but one of them said, "It looks like someone's ship came in!" I was stunned for a second and, hoping to motivate them, I said, "My ship never came in. I swam out and got it."

The problem was it didn't motivate them at all, and not long afterward, I started hearing that one by one, most of those old friends passed away with no dreams or goals. I think the difference between them and me was that I had asked Jesus to be the Lord of my life and guide me through this temporary, difficult world. I sure hope everyone I grew up with made the same decision at some point in their lives because it's the most important decision we will ever make to have life eternal in heaven.

Will you choose to get up and stay busy even when you don't feel like it, or will you choose to be a sluggard? Will you try to do everything on your own, or will you choose to ask Jesus to help you? Will you decide to have life eternal in Heaven? Each decision will have lifelong results!

1. Wine is a mocker, strong drink is raging, and whoever is deceived thereby is not wise.

2. The fear of a king is as the roaring of a lion; whoever provokes him to anger sins against his own soul.

3. It is an honor for a man to cease from strife, but every fool will be meddling.

4. The sluggard will not plow because of the cold; therefore, he shall beg in harvest and have nothing.

5. Counsel in the heart of man is like deep water, but a man of understanding will draw it out.

6. Most men will proclaim everyone his own goodness, but a faithful man who can find?

7. The just man walks in his integrity; his children are blessed after him.

8. A king that sits on the throne of judgment scatters away all evil with his eyes.

9. Who can say, I have made my heart clean, I am pure from my sin?

10. Diverse weights and measures are an abomination to the LORD.

11. Even a child is known by his doings, whether his work is pure and whether it is right.

12. The hearing ear and the seeing eye, the LORD made them both.

13. Love not sleep lest you come to poverty; open your eyes, and you shall be satisfied with bread.

14. It is naught, it is naught, says the buyer, but when he goes his way, then he boasts.

15. There is gold and a multitude of rubies, but the lips of knowledge are a precious jewel.

16. Take his garment that is surety for a stranger, and take a pledge of him for a strange woman.

17. Bread of deceit is sweet to a man but afterward his mouth will be filled with gravel.

18. Every purpose is established by counsel, and with good advice make war.

19. He that goes around as a talebearer reveals secrets; therefore, meddle not with him who flatters with his lips.

20. Whoever curses his father or his mother, his lamp shall be put out in obscure darkness.

21. An inheritance may be gotten hastily at the beginning, but the end thereof shall not be blessed.

22. Say not, I will recompense evil but wait on the LORD, and He will save you.

23. Diverse weights are an abomination unto the LORD, and a false balance is not good.

24. Man's goings are of the LORD; how can a man then understand his own way?

25. It is a snare to the man who devours that which is holy, and after vows to make inquiry.

26. A wise king scatters the wicked and brings the wheel over them.

27. The spirit of man is the candle of the LORD, searching all the inward parts of the belly.

28. Mercy and truth preserve the king, and his throne is upheld by mercy.

29. The glory of young men is their strength, and the beauty of old men is the gray head.

30. The blueness of a wound cleanses away evil, so do stripes the inward parts of the belly.

RIGHTEOUSNESS OVER SACRIFICE

Wisdom is what frees us to be our greater self.

— Mark Victor Hansen

We are reminded that diligence leads to plenteousness, but slothfulness not only leads to want, but it can also kill. We are reminded to be generous to the poor.

What has helped me countless times with various conflicts is this verse: "The king's heart is in the hand of the Lord; like the rivers of water, He turns it wherever He wishes" (Proverbs 21:1). You will find it comforting to remember that God controls even the king's heart. He even controls the heart of the most difficult person on earth. I hope you will find peace in difficult situations, knowing that God controls all hearts and outcomes. I encourage you to trust God with all difficult situations, people, and outcomes, no matter what the issues may be. Proverbs 3:5–6 states, "Trust in the Lord with all your heart and do not lean on your own understanding. In all your ways acknowledge Him, and He shall direct your paths."

Remember, God can speak to each of us differently through the same verses, so take the time to read this chapter slowly, pausing to consider any messages you sense are speaking directly to you.

1. The king's heart is in the hand of the LORD; like the rivers of water, He turns it whichever way He will.

2. Every way of a man is right in his own eyes, but the LORD ponders the heart.

3. To do justice and judgment is more acceptable to the LORD than sacrifice.

4. A high look, a proud heart, and the plowing of the wicked is sin.

5. The thoughts of the diligent tend only to plenteousness but of everyone that is hasty, only to want.

6. The getting of treasures by a lying tongue is a vanity tossed to and fro by them that seek death.

7. The robbery of the wicked shall destroy them because they refuse to do judgment.

8. The way of man is devious and strange, but as for the pure, his work is right.

9. It is better to dwell in a corner of the housetop than with a brawling woman in a wide house.

10. The soul of the wicked desires evil; his neighbor finds no favor in his eyes.

11. When the scorner is punished, the simple is made wise; and when the wise is instructed, he receives knowledge.

12. The righteous man wisely considers the house of the wicked, but God overthrows the wicked for their wickedness.

13. Whoever stops his ears at the cry of the poor, he will also cry himself, but shall not be heard.

14. A gift in secret pacifies anger and a reward in the bosom, strong wrath.

15. It is joy to the just to do judgment, but destruction shall be to the workers of iniquity.

16. The man that wanders out of the way of understanding shall remain in the congregation of the dead.

17. He that loves pleasure shall be a poor man; he that loves wine and oil shall not be rich.

18. The wicked shall be a ransom for the righteous and the transgressor for the upright.

19. It is better to dwell in the wilderness than with a contentious and angry woman.

20. There is treasure to be desired and oil in the dwelling of the wise, but a foolish man spends it up.

21. He that follows after righteousness and mercy finds life, righteousness, and honor.

22. A wise man scales the city of the mighty and casts down the strength of the confidence thereof.

23. Whoso keeps his mouth and his tongue keeps his soul from troubles.

24. Proud and haughty scorner is his name, who deals in proud wrath.

25. The desire of the slothful kills him, for his hands refuse to labor.

26. He covets greedily all day long, but the righteous gives and spares not.

27. The sacrifice of the wicked is an abomination; how much more, when he brings it with a wicked mind?

28. A false witness shall perish, but the man that hears, speaks constantly.

29. A wicked man hardens his face, but as for the upright, he directs his way.

30. There is no wisdom, nor understanding, nor counsel against the LORD.

31. The horse is prepared for the day of battle, but safety is from the LORD.

—

A GOOD NAME, TRAINING CHILDREN

A good name is more desirable than great riches.

— Proverbs 22:1

Choose a good name rather than great wealth! What a powerful opening statement and quite different than what we would typically think. You can do a lot of good with great wealth and riches. Some of the wealthiest people who ever walked the face of the earth are Bible heroes. I believe wealth can be used for good or for bad, and it's kind of like a brick. There's an old saying that goes like this, "A brick can be used to build a church, or it can be used to break a window."

Proverbs 22:4 confirms that God believes it's okay to have wealth and riches in saying, "By humility and fear of the Lord are riches and honor and life." If God says that, I'm all in! I don't know about you, but I am a giver by nature, and a giver must have something to give. I want to have enough finances not only to take care of my family's needs but also to help others in need.

Have you ever seen someone struggling at a grocery store cash register, counting pennies as they're trying to buy groceries and having to choose what they can keep or must put back? This is especially heart-wrenching if it's a single mother with hungry children around her or an elderly person not able to make ends meet.

This is becoming more of a normal occurrence, but I can't describe how incredible it feels to financially be able to walk over, put in your credit card, and pay their bill, seeking nothing in return. The best I can do is encourage you to do this and experience the unexplainable joy for yourself. I believe an abundant life would be what the apostle Paul describes in Galatians 5:22–23 as the fruits of the Spirit. These qualities are love, joy, peace, patience, kindness, goodness, faithfulness, gentleness, and self-control. I should do everything within my power to keep my name and reputation in good standing.

1. A good name is rather to be chosen than great riches and loving favor rather than silver and gold.

2. The rich and the poor meet together; the LORD is the maker of them all.

3. A prudent man foresees the evil and hides himself, but the simple pass on and are punished.

4. By humility and the fear of the LORD are riches, honor, and life.

5. Thorns and snares are in the way of the perverse, but he that keeps his soul shall be far from them.

6. Train up a child in the way he should go, and when he is old, he will not depart from it.

7. The rich rule over the poor, and the borrower is a servant to the lender.

8. He that sows iniquity shall reap vanity, and the rod of his anger shall fail.

9. He that has a bountiful eye shall be blessed, for he gives of his bread to the poor.

10. Cast out the scorner and contention shall go out; yes, strife and reproach shall cease.

11. He that loves pureness of heart, for the grace of his lips, the king shall be his friend.

12. The eyes of the LORD preserve knowledge, and He overthrows the words of the transgressor.

13. The slothful man says, there is a lion outside, I shall be slain in the streets.

14. The mouths of strange women are a deep pit, and he that is abhorred by the LORD shall fall therein.

15. Foolishness is bound in the heart of a child, but the rod of correction shall drive it far from him.

16. He that oppresses the poor to increase his riches, and he that gives to the rich shall surely come to want.

17. Bow down your ear, hear the words of the wise, and apply your heart unto My knowledge.

18. For it is a pleasant thing if you keep them within you; they shall be fitted in your lips.

19. That your trust may be in the LORD, I have made known to you this day, even to you.

20. Have I not written to you excellent things in counsels and knowledge,

21. That I might make you know the certainty of the words of truth; that you might answer the words of truth to those who send unto you?

22. Rob not the poor because he is poor; neither oppress the afflicted in the gate.

23. For the LORD will plead their cause and spoil the soul of those that spoiled them.

24. Make no friendship with an angry man, and with a furious man you shall not go;

25. Lest you learn his ways and get a snare to your soul.

26. Be not one of them that strike hands nor of them that are sureties for debts.

27. If you have nothing to pay, why should he take away your bed from under you?

28. Remove not the ancient landmark which your fathers have set.

29. See a man diligent in his business? He shall stand before kings; he shall not stand before mean men.

—

RESTRAINT & CONTENTMENT

Why are you so busy with this or that….

— Rumi

If I was asked to think back to my early years of reading the book of Proverbs, about how this chapter impacted me, I would have to say there were several key verses that stood out and made me feel as though God were speaking directly to me. This chapter focuses on being wise and how respecting your parents will make them happy. My dad used to say to me, "Gerry put your hand in front of your face and look at it. That's as far as you can see. God, on the other hand, can see all the way down all roads and will lead you to the fruitful direction of your destiny."

I truly believed, since I was under their roof and they were paying my bills, I needed to place myself under my parents' authority. When I graduated high school and started college, they continued to pay my bills even when I moved three hundred miles away to Atlanta, Georgia, to attend Life University's Chiropractic College. All I had to do was be respectful, follow their rules (which were minimal), and do my very best in college, and they continued to support my goals. My parents weren't wealthy, but they were both Chiropractors and so was my grandfather, an uncle, and one cousin before me. My parents were thrilled that I decided to become a Chiropractor. After I graduated, two brothers, a sister, a brother-in-law, and a bunch of cousins also became Chiropractors. I feel total contentment as I write this book to share my story in hopes that it will inspire your ever-better story.

1. When you sit to eat with a ruler, consider diligently what is before you;

2. And put a knife to your throat if you are a man given to appetite.

3. Do not desire his dainties for they are deceitful food.

4. Labor not to be rich and cease from your own wisdom.

5. Will you set your eyes upon that which is not? For riches certainly make themselves wings, and they fly away as an eagle toward heaven.

6. Eat not the bread of him that has an evil eye, neither desire his dainty food;

7. For as he thinks in his heart, so is he. Eat and drink, he says to you, but his heart is not with you.

8. The morsel which you have eaten shall you vomit up and lose your sweet words.

9. Speak not in the ears of a fool, for he will despise the wisdom of your words.

10. Remove not the old landmark and enter not into the fields of the fatherless;

11. For their Redeemer is mighty, and He will plead their cause with you.

12. Apply your heart unto instruction and your ears to the words of knowledge.

13. Withhold not correction from the child, for if you beat him with the rod, he shall not die.

14. You shall beat him with the rod and deliver his soul from hell.

15. My son, if your heart is wise, my heart shall rejoice, even mine.

16. Yes, my heart shall rejoice when your lips say the right things.

17. Let not your heart envy sinners but fear the LORD all day long.

18. For surely there is an end, and your expectation shall not be cut off.

19. Hear my son, be wise and guide your heart in the way.

20. Be not among winebibbers and riotous eaters of flesh;

21. For the drunkard and the glutton shall come to poverty and drowsiness shall clothe a man with rags.

22. Listen to your father that begot you and despise not your mother when she is old.

23. Buy the truth and sell it not; also, wisdom, instruction, and understanding.

24. The father of the righteous shall greatly rejoice, and he that begets a wise child shall have joy of him.

25. Your father and your mother will be glad, and she that bore you shall rejoice.

26. My son, give me your heart and let your eyes observe my ways.

27. For a harlot is a deep ditch, and a strange woman is a narrow pit.

28. She lies in wait as for a prey and increases the transgressors among men.

29. Who has sadness? Who has sorrow? Who has contentions? Who has babbling? Who has wounds without cause? Who has redness of eyes?

30. Those who tarry long at the wine and those that seek mixed wine.

31. Look not upon the wine when it is red, when it gives its color in the cup, when it moves itself aright.

32. At the last, it bites like a serpent and stings like an adder.

33. Your eyes shall behold strange women, and your heart shall utter perverse things.

34. Yes, you shall be like he that lies down in the middle of the sea or like he that lies upon the top of a mast.

35. They have stricken me, you will say, and I was not sick; they have beaten me, and I felt it not. When will I awaken? I will seek it again.

—

WISDOM IN ADVERSITY

Kites rise highest against the wind, not with it.

— Winston Churchill

A wise man is strong in spirit, mind, and body. We are also taught "in the multitude of counselors, there is safety" (Proverbs 11:14). We are taught not to fear evil men or envy the wicked.

We are taught not to rejoice when our enemy stumbles because if God sees it, and He will, it will displease Him, and He will turn His wrath away from our enemy and onto us. It will cause a boomerang effect and come back on us.

Solomon teaches us to build our business before we build our house. My grandfather and father used to call that "putting the cart before the horse." When I asked my father, he said, "Think about it, Gerry. Picture a cart in front of a horse." So, as Proverbs 24:27 simply implies, it is wise to build your business before you build your house.

This is all vital information in the path to gaining wisdom and its rewards, but the most important parts of this chapter that really made me think long and hard were the last verses, 31–34. Solomon, who I'm convinced believed slothfulness is very destructive, draws the perfect unforgettable picture of how a life of laziness or slothfulness will end. The picture he drew in my mind is so vivid and clear, it still flashes in my mind at times and motivates me to remain diligent in all that I do.

Read verses 30–34 slowly, absorb the warnings, and allow the mental pictures to be permanently stamped in your mind. Trust me, the picture is real, and, if you choose, it can help prevent a potentially disastrous ending.

1. Be not envious of evil men, neither desire to be with them;

2. For their heart studies destruction, and their lips talk of mischief.

3. Through wisdom a house is built, by understanding it is established;

4. And by knowledge, the chambers shall be filled with all precious and pleasant riches.

5. A wise man is strong, yes, a man of knowledge increases strength.

6. By wise counsel you shall make your war, and in the multitude of counselors, there is safety.

7. Wisdom is too high for a fool; he opens not his mouth in the gate.

8. He that devises to do evil shall be called a mischievous person.

9. The thought of foolishness is sin, and the scorner is an abomination to men.

10. If you faint in the day of adversity, your strength is small.

11. If you don't deliver them that are drawn unto death and those that are ready to be slain;

12. If you say we knew it not, does not He that ponders the heart consider it? And He that keeps your soul, does He not know it? And shall He not render to every man according to his works?

13. My son, eat honey because it is good and the honeycomb, which is sweet to your taste;

14. So shall the knowledge of wisdom be to your soul; when you have found it, then there shall be a reward, and your expectation shall not be cut off.

15. Lay not waiting, O wicked man, against the dwelling of the righteous; spoil not his resting place;

16. For a just man falls seven times and rises again, but the wicked shall fall into mischief.

17. Rejoice not when your enemy falls and let not your heart be glad when he stumbles;

18. Lest the LORD see it, it displeases Him, and He turns away His wrath from him.

19. Fret not thyself because of evil men, neither be envious of the wicked;

20. For there shall be no reward to the evil man, and the candle of the wicked shall be put out.

21. My son, fear the LORD and the king, and meddle not with them that are given to change;

22. For their calamity shall rise suddenly, and who knows the ruin of them both?

23. These things also belong to the wise. It is not good to have respect of persons in judgment.

24. He that says to the wicked, you are righteous, the people will curse and nations shall abhor him;

25. But to those that rebuke him shall be delight, and a good blessing shall come upon them.

26. Every man shall kiss the lips that give a right answer.

27. Prepare you work without, make it fit for yourself in the field, and afterward build your house.

28. Be not a witness against your neighbor without cause and deceive not with your lips.

29. Say not, I will do unto him as he has done unto me; I will render to the man according to his work.

30. I went by the field of the slothful and by the vineyard of the man void of understanding;

31. And it was all overgrown with thorns, nettles had covered the face of it, and the stone wall was broken down.

32. Then I saw and considered it well. I looked upon it and received instruction.

33. Yes, a little sleep, a little slumber, a little folding of the hands to sleep;

34. So shall your poverty come as one that travels and
     your want as an armed man.

115

—

WORDS FITLY SPOKEN

Good words are worth much and cost little.

— George Herbert

We are all works in progress.

I am sitting on a breathtaking bluff overlooking what we grew up calling "the Wappoo Cut." It is part of the Intercoastal Waterway that runs between James Island and West Ashley in Charleston, South Carolina. It is such a beautiful, peaceful, and loving place where I could be in touch with God and positively transform my life and future. We all need a place of refuge like this where we can decompress. I've spent many quiet hours on this river and bluff, watching the boats travel north and south. I was always contemplating where I had been, where I am, and where I wanted to go in life.

When I am troubled and need peace, the Holy Spirit reminds me to "be still and know that I am God" (Psalm 46:10). I hear the still, small voice of the Holy Spirit giving me guidance.

The next time you are deeply troubled or don't know what to do in a particular situation, please remember God wants you to come into the stillness where you will find His presence and know Him. I promise you will have the wonderful peace of God wash over you, lift you up, and give you that peace. It will let you know you are loved and set you free.

1. These are also proverbs of Solomon, which the men of Hezekiah, king of Judah, copied out.

2. It is the glory of God to conceal a thing, but the honor of kings is to search out a matter.

3. The heaven for height, the earth for depth, and the hearts of kings are unsearchable.

4. Take away the dross from the silver and there shall come forth a vessel for the refiner.

5. Take away the wicked from before the king and his throne shall be established in righteousness.

6. Do not put yourself in the presence of the king and do not stand in the place of great men;

7. For it is better that it be said to you, come up here, than that you should be put lower in the presence of the prince, whom your eyes have seen.

8. Do not go hastily to strive, lest you know not what to do in the end, when your neighbor has put you to shame.

9. Debate your cause with your neighbor privately and divulge not a secret to another;

10. Lest he that hears it put you to shame and your infamy turn not away.

11. A word fitly spoken is like apples of gold in pictures of silver.

12. As an earring of gold, and an ornament of fine gold, so is a wise reprover upon an obedient ear.

13. As the cold of snow in the time of harvest, so is a faithful messenger to them that send him; for he refreshes the soul of his masters.

14. Whoever boasts himself of a false gift is like clouds and wind without rain.

15. By long forbearing is a prince persuaded, and a soft tongue breaks the bone.

16. Have you found honey? Eat as much is sufficient for you, lest you be filled therewith, and vomit it.

17. Withdraw your foot from your neighbor's house lest he be weary of you and hate you.

18. A man that bears false witness against his neighbor is a maul, a sword, and a sharp arrow.

19. Confidence in an unfaithful man, in times of trouble, is like a broken tooth and a foot out of joint.

20. As he that takes away a garment in cold weather and as vinegar upon soda, so is he that sings songs to a heavy heart.

21. If your enemy is hungry, give him bread to eat, and if he is thirsty, give him water to drink;

22. For you will heap coals of fire upon his head, and the LORD will reward you.

23. The north wind drives away rain, so does an angry countenance a backbiting tongue.

24. It is better to dwell in the corner of the housetop than with a brawling woman in a wide house.

25. As cold water to a thirsty soul, so is good news from a faraway country.

26. A righteous man falling before the wicked is like a troubled fountain and a corrupt spring.

27. It is not good to eat too much honey, so for men to search their own glory, is not glory.

28. He that has no rule over his own spirit is like a city that is broken down without walls.

—

FOLLY UNMASKED

Thanks are the highest form of thought.

— G. K. Chesterton

Solomon wisely taught here, "Where there is no wood, the fire goes out" (Proverbs 26:20).

Have you ever had a conflict with someone, and it seemed like the arguing never stopped because both people wanted to be right? Sometimes these arguments can go on for days, possibly months or even years. Talk about damaging. Wow! These kinds of conflicts can leave deep scars, but my dad had a couple of statements I later learned were verses directly out of Proverbs, telling me how to clear up conflicts. One of the best ways he taught me was by asking a question like, "Gerry, how do you clear up a glass of muddy water?"

He'd always pause to make me think about the question, and then he'd tell me how to do the thing he was referring to. In this case, he said, "Well, you simply stop stirring it." Stop "stirring" an argument, and it will end.

Like the verse above, stop putting wood on the fire, and the fire will go out.

He also quoted Proverbs 17:14 often: "The beginning of strife is like when one lets out water; therefore, leave off contention, before it is meddled with." The points are clear: Just don't argue! Let the dust settle and let things clear up. Dad was right. They always would with time. Like Solomon said, "A fool tells everything he knows, but a wise man keeps his mouth shut" (paraphrased Proverbs 17:28).

1. As snow in summer and rain in harvest, so honor is not seemly for a fool.

2. As the bird by wandering, as the swallow by flying, so the causeless curse shall not come.

3. A whip for the horse, a bridle for the ass, and a rod for the fool's back.

4. Answer not a fool according to his folly, lest you also be like him.

5. Answer a fool according to his folly, lest he be wise in his own conceit.

6. He that sends a message by the hand of a fool cuts off the feet and drinks damage.

7. The legs of the lame are not equal, so is a parable in the mouth of fools.

8. As he that binds a stone in a sling, so is he that gives honor to a fool.

9. As a thorn goes up into the hand of a drunkard, so is a parable in the mouth of fools.

10. The great God that formed all things rewards both the fool and the transgressors.

11. As a dog returns to his vomit, so a fool returns to his folly.

12. See a man wise in his own conceit? There is more hope of a fool than of him.

13. The slothful man says, there is a lion in the way; a lion is in the streets.

14. As the door turns upon its hinges, so does the slothful upon his bed.

15. The slothful hides his hand in his bosom; it grieves him to bring it to his mouth again.

16. The sluggard is wiser in his own conceit than seven men that can render a reason.

17. He that passes by and meddles with strife, not belonging to him, is like one that takes a dog by the ears.

18. As a mad man who casts firebrands, arrows and death;

19. So is the man that deceives his neighbor and says, am I not in sport?

20. Where no wood is, the fire goes out; so, where there is no talebearer, the strife ceases.

21. As coals are to burning coals, and wood to fire, so is a contentious man to kindle strife.

22. The words of a talebearer are as wounds, and they go down into the innermost parts of the belly.

23. Burning lips and a wicked heart are like broken pottery covered with silver dross.

24. He that hates dissembles with his lips and lays up deceit within himself.

25. When he speaks pleasantly, believe him not, for there are seven abominations in his heart;

26. Whose hatred is covered by deceit; his wickedness shall be shown before the whole congregation.

27. Whoever digs a pit shall fall therein, and he that rolls a stone, it will return upon him.

28. A lying tongue hates those that are afflicted by it, and a flattering mouth works ruin.

—

FRIENDSHIP, IRON SHARPENS IRON

*Motivation gets you going, but discipline
keeps you growing.*

— John C. Maxwell

Have you ever been so excited about something that I could possibly happen in the future that you told everybody about it? I know I have. Bursting with excitement in the wrong place at the wrong time caused me chagrin. It wasn't intentional. I didn't really mean to brag about it. I got caught up in the possibilities, and I told others about it before it happened, and that's never a good idea. The problem is, if it doesn't come true, the ridicule and embarrassment are sometimes unbearable.

When I was much younger, probably four or five years old, my father used to take us camping at the beach, which was cool at night. I got it into my mind that I wanted to go camping at the beach again.

At the age of twelve, I begged and pleaded with my dad to take us to the beach to camp out. Dad just couldn't find the time. He was over fifty by then, and he no longer wanted to be cold at night on the beach.

My grandfather was coming to visit us for Thanksgiving. When Grandad called to confirm he was coming, I heard mom talking to him and asked if I could talk to him. I knew I could persuade him to take us to the beach. I was an invincible twelve-year-old. My mother handed me the phone, and I began pleading with him to take my best friend and me camping at the beach. He didn't say no, but he absolutely didn't say yes.

I had a good relationship with my grandfather. I just assumed that he'd love to take us camping at the beach. I told my best friend who camped out with me behind the house every Friday night, "We're going camping at the beach, so pack your bags." I had a big duffel bag, and I packed it with everything I could think of possibly needing on a day or two camping trip. My friend came over a couple of times in the following week, and he saw all my stuff packed up. He asked if I was sure we were going. I just couldn't imagine my grandfather letting me down, so I had my friend get his things ready to go. I suspect my friend then told all our friends that we were going camping at the beach.

The day came that my grandfather arrived, but when I mentioned camping at the beach, he looked at me with a blank stare, as though we had never had the conversation at all. He finally let me know that we weren't going to the beach. I was crushed, but the worst part of it all was that I had my friend convinced we were going, and he had been telling everyone else.

You know, this chapter opened with a relative verse that spoke volumes to me later in life. Proverbs 27:1 states, "Do not boast about tomorrow, for you do not know what a day may bring forth."

The second verse also had a profound impact on my life. Proverbs 27:2 states, "Let another man praise you, and not your own mouth." I thought after I had graduated college that I needed to introduce myself as Dr. Gerry Fox. Belinda and I were newlyweds and visiting churches around San Francisco, California, where I first practiced. We were visiting a church, and a pastor asked all the visitors to stand up and introduce themselves. When it was my turn, I said, "I'm Dr. Gerry Fox, and this is my wife, Belinda." You could almost feel the discomfort in the congregation, and looking back, it was probably because I was unintentionally making myself out to be more important or better than others, which had never entered my consciousness. I just didn't have the awareness to know how to handle this new title. Well, Belinda knew how to handle it and let me know later.

Belinda loves people. She is very sweet, and if you are blessed to meet her someday, she'll be your best friend in three minutes. When you leave her, your life will be better for having spent time with her.

When we got in the car, Belinda sweetly asked me, "Why do you feel the need to introduce yourself as Dr. Fox?" I tried my best to squirm out of the awkwardness, but it was impossible because she was right. She said, "It's better not to announce your title but that you are simply Gerry Fox, which is what you were before you had that 'Dr.' in front of your name. If you introduce yourself by your first name, people will feel more comfortable around you, and you will appear far more important when they find out you are a doctor."

I think we all want to feel important, and that's okay, but what's more important is to make others feel important. There was a famous quote by Dale Carnegie in his book *How to Win Friends and Influence People*. The quote goes like this, "If you want to have enemies, excel your friends, but if you want to have friends, let your friends excel you." If you have never read this book, I highly recommend you pick it up and read it.

1. Boast not about tomorrow, for you know not what a day may bring forth.

2. Let another man praise you, and not your own mouth, a stranger and not your own lips.

3. A stone is heavy, and the sand weighty, but a fool's wrath is heavier than them both.

4. Wrath is cruel and anger is outrageous, but who is able to stand before envy?

5. Open rebuke is better than secret love.

6. Faithful are the wounds of a friend, but the kisses of an enemy are deceitful.

7. The full soul loathes a honeycomb, but to the hungry soul, every bitter thing is sweet.

8. As a bird that wanders from her nest, so is a man that wanders from his place.

9. Ointment and perfume rejoice the heart; so does the sweetness of a man's friend by hearty counsel.

10. Your own friend and your father's friend, forsake not; neither go into your brother's house in the day of thy calamity; for better is a neighbor that is near than a brother far off.

11. My son, be wise and make my heart glad, that I may answer him that reproaches me.

12. A prudent man foresees the evil and hides himself, but the simple pass on and are punished.

13. Take his garment that is surety for a stranger and take a pledge of him for a strange woman.

14. He that blesses his friend with a loud voice, rising early in the morning, it shall be counted a curse to him.

15. A continual dropping, in a very rainy day, and a contentious woman are alike;

16. Whoever hides her hides the wind and the ointment of his right hand will betray him.

17. Iron sharpens iron, so a man sharpens the countenance of his friend.

18. Whoever keeps the fig tree shall eat the fruit, so he that waits on his master shall be honored.

19. As in water, face answers to face, so the heart of man to man.

20. Hell and destruction are never full, so the eyes of man are never satisfied.

21. As the fining pot for silver, and the furnace for gold, so is a man to his praise.

22. Though you crush a fool in a mortar, among wheat with a pestle, yet his foolishness will not depart from him.

23. Be diligent to know the state of your flocks and look well to your herds.

24. For riches are not forever, and does the crown endure to every generation?

25. The hay appears, the tender grass shows itself, and the herbs of the mountains are gathered.

26. The lambs are for your clothing; the goats are the price of the field;

27. And you shall have enough goats' milk for your food, for the food of your household, and for the maintenance of your maidens.

—

BOLDNESS
OF THE RIGHTEOUS

Here I stand; I can do no other.

— Martin Luther

I mentioned how the book of Proverbs has led me to achieve greater success. Verse 19 of this chapter says, "He who tills his land shall have plenty of bread." That means when you work and take the initiative to take action in your business, you will prosper greatly.

As a Chiropractor, I listened to all the doctors who were helping over a hundred patients a day and saw that they manifested ever greater healing powers as well as money-making abilities. Seeing a lot of patients stimulates your healing power and prowess. Plus, they were rewarded with more success, accolades, and great friendships. I was inspired and experienced the same. In verse 20, Solomon continues, "A faithful man shall abound with blessings." This is what happens when you get onto the path of your divine destiny and purposefully move forward with desire, confidence, and joy. And when we have abundance, we should joyfully share with those who are in need.

Mark Victor Hansen told me of an experience that he wanted to share on this subject. His wife Crystal and he were in the checkout line at the grocery store. Behind them was a father with three small hungry children. The little boy politely and innocently asked his father if he could buy them some milk. "Please, dad," the little boy said.

His dad lovingly said, "Son, that's not in our budget tonight."

As Mark drove away, the thought of what he'd just experienced nagged at him. He had wanted to hand the man money for the milk, but he thought he might embarrass the man or hurt his dignity. All the way home, he thought about how he could easily have slipped a twenty-dollar bill out of his pocket, dropped it on the floor, picked it up, winked, and said to the man, "I think you dropped this," allowing the man to keep his dignity and solve the problem. While hurting at the thought of hungry children, he declared to himself, "I'll never let that happen again."

Shortly after that incident, Kelly, their daughter who teaches 120 special needs kids daily, said, "Mom and Dad, because the government shut down for forty-three days, some of my kids are starving. They come to school so hungry. My teacher's salary hardly covers my monthly expenses. Would you please help and buy them Chomp Meat Sticks at Costco? They love those, and it provides good protein for them."

Mark said, "None of my children or the children under their watch shall ever be hungry. Tell me how many you need, and I'll buy them tomorrow at Costco and get them to you." Now each month he checks in with his daughter to see what snack needs she has for the children at school. Nothing makes him happier.

1. The wicked flee when no man pursues, but the righteous are bold as a lion.

2. For the transgression of a land, many are the princes thereof, but by a man of understanding and knowledge, the state thereof shall be prolonged.

3. A poor man that oppresses the poor is like a sweeping rain which leaves no food.

4. They that forsake the law praise the wicked, but those who keep the law contend with them.

5. Evil men understand not judgment, but they that seek the LORD understand all things.

6. Better is the poor that walks in his uprightness than he that is rich and perverse in his ways.

7. Whoever keeps the law is a wise son, but he who is a companion of riotous men shames his father.

8. He that by usury and unjust gain increases his substance, shall gather it for him that will pity the poor.

9. He that turns away his ear from hearing the law, even his prayer shall be an abomination.

10. Whoever causes the righteous to go astray in an evil way shall fall into his own pit, but the upright shall have good things in possession.

11. The rich man is wise in his own conceit, but the poor that has understanding searches him out.

12. When righteous men rejoice, there is great glory; but when the wicked rise, a man is hidden.

13. He that covers his sins shall not prosper, but whoever confesses and forsakes them shall have mercy.

14. Happy is the man that fears always, but he that hardens his heart shall fall into mischief.

15. As a roaring lion and a ranging bear, so is a wicked ruler over the poor.

16. The prince that lacks understanding is also a great oppressor, but he that hates covetousness shall prolong his days.

17. A man that does violence to the blood of any person shall flee to the pit; let no man sustain him.

18. Whoso walks uprightly shall be saved but he that is perverse in his ways shall fall at once.

19. He that tills his land shall have plenty of bread, but he that follows vain persons shall have poverty enough.

20. A faithful man shall abound with blessings, but he that makes haste to be rich shall not be innocent.

21. Having respect of persons is not good because for a piece of bread that man will transgress.

22. He that hastens to be rich has an evil eye and considers not that poverty shall come upon him.

23. He that rebukes a man afterward shall find more favor than he that flatters with the tongue.

24. Whoever robs his father or his mother and says it is no transgression; the same is the companion of a destroyer.

25. He that has a proud heart stirs up strife, but he that puts his trust in the LORD shall be made fat.

26. He that trusts in his own heart is a fool, but whoever walks wisely shall be delivered.

27. He that gives to the poor shall not lack, but he that hides his eyes shall have many curses.

28. When the wicked rise, men hide themselves, but when they perish, the righteous increase.

—

VISION, JUSTICE, RESTRAINT

Where there is no vision of God, people perish.

— Proverbs 29:18

Herein, Solomon makes the famous quote that we've all heard so many times, "Where there is no vision, the people perish." I have listened to motivational speakers for insight, inspiration, and guidance for over fifty years, and honestly, I don't know one of them who hasn't quoted this same verse from Proverbs 29:18. I believe the reason this is true is because the greatest minds on the planet understand the detrimental reality of having no vision for your life.

I heard a story one time from a motivational speaker, who told about a traveler who stopped at a gas station for directions. The attendant asked one simple question, "Where are you going?"

The driver said, "I don't know."

The attendant said, "Well, sir, if you don't know where you're going, how am I supposed to tell you how to get there?"

It's like having dreams and goals. If you can't see it, you can't achieve it or get there. Psalm 37:4 states, "Delight yourself also in the LORD, and He shall give you the desires of your heart." The Bible also states in James 1:17, "Every good and every perfect gift is from above and comes down from the Father of lights, with whom there is no variation or shadow of turning." I believe this verse indicates that all spiritual and physical blessings come from God.

What are your dreams? Dreams give you a directional compass. When your goals are in writing, they become your lifelong GPS. Do you have any dreams or goals? Are they in writing? Or are you just floundering through life hoping everything's going to turn out well.

We need dreams, and like Belinda jokingly told me when we first got married, "Gerry, all you need to buy me is a plantation." Belinda is a true southern lady, very gracious and always put together. Was she serious about the plantation? Probably not, but if it worked out, she'd be very excited. Honestly, it is still one of my dreams to own and live on a large piece of property. That sounds like an outrageous goal or a dream, but if someone can have a plantation, anyone can have a plantation. Since I said, "I do," we have been blessed so abundantly from three wonderful adult children, two amazing sons-in-law, an amazing daughter-in-law, and now ten extraordinary grandchildren.

Do yourself a great favor, take some time to write out what you want out of life, how many children you want, what kind of house you want to live in, what kind of income you want, how much freedom you want in your life, how many ministries you want to support, and how many people you want to help. These are your dreams between you and God alone, and it doesn't matter how big, outrageous, or bodacious they are. I've always heard the bigger and more outrageous your dreams and goals are, the better, but write them down. Read over them morning and night by saying them, seeing them, and feeling them. What does it *feel* like to have those dreams come true? How many people would you like to help? How many missionaries, missions, ministries, and churches would you like to support? Who is in need that you are now able to help, whether it's spiritually, morally, financially, or physically?

1. He that is often reproved hardens his neck and shall suddenly be destroyed without remedy.

2. When the righteous are in authority, the people rejoice, but when the wicked rule, the people mourn.

3. Whoever loves wisdom rejoices his father, but he that keeps company with harlots spends his substance.

4. The king by judgment establishes the land, but he that receives gifts overthrows it.

5. A man that flatters his neighbor spreads a net for his feet.

6. In the transgression of an evil man there is a snare, but the righteous sing and rejoice.

7. The righteous consider the cause of the poor, but the wicked prefer not to know it.

8. Scornful men bring a city into a snare, but wise men turn away wrath.

9. If a wise man contends with a foolish man, whether he rage or laugh, there is no rest.

10. The bloodthirsty hate the upright, but the just seek his soul.

11. A fool utters all his mind, but a wise man keeps it in till afterwards.

12. If a ruler harkens to lies, all his servants are wicked.

13. The poor and the deceitful man meet together; the LORD lightens both their eyes.

14. The king that faithfully judges the poor, his throne shall be established forever.

15. The rod and reproof give wisdom, but a child left to himself brings his mother to shame.

16. When the wicked are multiplied, transgression increases, but the righteous shall see their fall.

17. Correct your son and he will give you rest; yes, he will delight your soul.

18. Where there is no vision, the people perish, but he that keeps the law is happy.

19. A servant cannot be corrected by words, for though he understands, he will not answer.

20. Do you see a man that is hasty in his words? There is more hope of a fool than of him.

21. He that delicately brings up his servant from a child, shall have him become his son at the length.

22. An angry man stirs up strife, and a furious man abounds in transgression.

23. A man's pride will bring him low, but honor will uphold the humble in spirit.

24. Whoever is partner with a thief hates his own soul; he hears cursing and does not condemn it.

25. The fear of man brings a snare, but whoever puts his trust in the LORD shall be safe.

26. Many seek the ruler's favor, but every man's judgment comes from the LORD.

27. An unjust man is an abomination to the just, and he that is upright in the way is an abomination to the wicked.

HUMILITY & LIMITS OF KNOWLEDGE

If you want to change the world, go home and
love your family.

— Mother Teresa

King Solomon had the insight to know in advance that God has a Son (Jesus). Solomon refers to God and His Son in Proverbs 30:4: "Who has ascended up into Heaven or descended? Who has gathered the wind in His fists? Who has bound the waters in a garment? Who has established all the ends of the earth? What is His name, and what is His Son's name, if you can tell?"

Today, I am compelled to include some truths that may not have a direct relationship to this Proverb. I believe these are very important. I have done my very best to literally be an instrument for God to speak through to you, so I don't question what I'm writing when I feel strongly about including it.

I learned much through reading the book of Proverbs throughout my life. Proverbs 13:20 states, "He who walks with wise men shall be wise, but a companion of fools shall be destroyed." One of these incredible wise leaders is my friend, Mark Victor Hansen, who is helping create this book.

Mark would agree with me that there is one relationship that is so much more important than any relationship we can have here during our short time on Earth. How would you like to have a personal relationship with the *One* who created the Heavens and the Earth and everything in it? I think a lot of people have no idea that they can have a close personal relationship with the Holy Trinity, our Maker: God the Father, God the Son, and the Holy Spirit.

We can have a true relationship with our Maker by simply asking. We then do our part to read our Bible and pray without ceasing, like the apostle Paul said. Consider praying when you wake up in the morning, just before you go to sleep, or any time you feel the need. Take time to pause for a quick prayer before every meeting and bless whomever you are meeting. Mark imagines a soothing pink light surrounding each person in the meeting he is entering, and the meetings go magnificently well.

I hope and pray that as you read the book of Proverbs, it will simply give you a segue to the pages of the entire Bible, sometimes referred to as "God's love letter to his children."

Do you choose to walk through the maze of this life alone, or will you choose to have a personal relationship with the Creator of the universe?

I chose to have a personal relationship with God, Jesus, and the Holy Spirit many years ago, and my life has been blessed abundantly since. I don't know how anyone walks through life without taking advantage of this incredible opportunity to be close friends with God.

God has open arms and welcomes all to Him. It is a simple choice, and it is yours alone to make.

1. The words of Agur the son of Jakeh, even the prophecy. The man spoke unto Ithiel, even unto Ithiel and Ucal.

2. Surely, I am dumber than any man and have not the understanding of a man.

3. I neither learned wisdom nor have the knowledge of the Holy One.

4. Who has ascended up into heaven, or descended? Who has gathered the wind in His fists? Who has bound the waters in a garment? Who has established all the ends of the earth? What is His name, and what is His Son's name, if you can tell?

5. Every word of God is pure; He is a shield to them that put their trust in Him.

6. Do not add to His words, lest He reprove you and you are found to be a liar.

7. Two things I have required of you; do not deny them to me before I die.

8. Remove vanity and lies far from me, give me neither poverty nor riches, and feed me with food convenient for me;

9. Lest I be full, deny you, and say, who is the LORD? Or lest I be poor, steal, and take the name of my God in vain.

10. Accuse not a servant to his master, lest he curse you, and you be found guilty.

11. There is a generation that curses their father and does not bless their mother.

12. There is a generation that is pure in their own eyes and yet is not washed from their filthiness.

13. There is a generation, O how lofty are their eyes! And their eyelids are lifted up.

14. There is a generation whose teeth are as swords and their jaw teeth as knives, to devour the poor from off the earth and the needy from among men.

15. The horseleech has two daughters, crying, "Give, give." There are three things that are never satisfied, yes, four things say not, it is enough;

16. The grave, the barren womb, the earth that is not filled with water, and the fire that says not, it is enough.

17. The eye that mocks at his father and despises to obey his mother, the ravens of the valley will pick it out, and the young eagles shall eat it.

18. There are three things which are too wonderful for me, yes, four which I know not;

19. The way of an eagle in the air, the way of a serpent upon a rock, the way of a ship in the midst of the sea, and the way of a man with a maid.

20. Such is the way of an adulterous woman; she eats, wipes her mouth, and says, I have done no wickedness.

21. For three things the earth is disquieted and for four which it cannot bear:

22. For a servant when he reigns, a fool when he is filled with food,

23. For an odious woman when she is married, and a handmaid that is heir to her mistress.

24. There are four things which are little upon the earth, but they are exceedingly wise.

25. The ants are a people not strong, yet they prepare their food in the summer.

26. The conies are feeble folk, yet they make their houses in the rocks.

27. The locusts have no king, yet all of them go forth by bands.

28. The spider takes hold with her hands and is in kings' palaces.

29. There are three things which go well, yes, four are comely in going;

30. A lion which is strongest among beasts and turns not away for any,

31. A greyhound, a he goat also, and a king, against whom there is no rising up.

32. If you have done foolishly in lifting up yourself, or if you have thought evil, put your hand over your mouth.

33. Surely the churning of milk produces butter, and the wringing of the nose produces blood; so the forcing of wrath brings forth strife.

NOBLE CHARACTER

Well done is better than well said.

— Benjamin Franklin

I can't count the number of times my father would encourage me to look for a wife like the woman in Proverbs 31. It wasn't the only time, but his encouragement usually followed a breakup with a girlfriend. It was usually a woman I thought I loved who was pretty, too, but who didn't see us having a future together. I was usually the one who was hurt and crushed because the ladies usually had other ideas. The reason I say this is because reading this chapter made me want to find the best wife like the one Proverbs 31 guided me to. I would pray, "God, if this isn't the woman that you think is best for my life-long partner, will you please remove her from my life?" God always answered that prayer.

I always prayed and asked God to bring me the right wife for my life. Were these times painful? Yes, but looking back, I'm so thankful God intervened and did not allow me to marry any of those great young ladies because I would have missed God's incredible gift of Belinda, our three wonderful children, and our ten grandchildren. Belinda is beyond precious to me.

Belinda and I grew up six hundred miles apart. We had a telephone romance. I had invited her to visit me in my hometown of Charleston, South Carolina. Belinda loved history. The first day of her stay, I was tied up all day taking my South Carolina Chiropractic board test. My father loved showing people around this incredible historic city and was given the honor and privilege of giving her the insider's tour. He basically spent the entire day one-on-one with Belinda. Late that night, around 1:00 a.m., after the family dinner and other planned events, my father came into my room, picked up my Bible, handed it to me, and choked up with tears in his eyes as he said, "Gerry, Belinda meets every one of those characteristics in Proverbs 31."

Wow! I guess God was giving His approval!

The other side of this is that ever since he told me to read this chapter over and over, I would always ask him what he thought about my girlfriends, and although he liked them all, his answer was usually something like, "We'll see," or, "Let's give it some time," but this was completely different. In my honest opinion, this was just God using my father to make it real that this was His choice of a Proverbs 31 wife, Belinda.

1. These are the words of King Lemuel, the prophecy that his mother taught him.

2. What, my son? And what, the son of my womb? And what, the son of my vows?

3. Give not your strength to women, nor your ways to that which destroys kings.

4. It is not for kings, O Lemuel, it is not for kings to drink wine, nor for princes strong drink;

5. Lest they drink, forget the law, and pervert the judgment of any of the afflicted.

6. Give strong drink to him that is ready to perish and wine to those with a heavy heart.

7. Let him drink, forget his poverty, and remember his misery no more.

8. Open your mouth for the dumb, in the cause of all, who are appointed to destruction.

9. Open your mouth, judge righteously, and plead the cause of the poor and needy.

10. Who can find a virtuous woman? For her price is far above rubies.

11. The heart of her husband safely trusts in her so that he shall have no need of spoil.

12. She will do him good and not evil all the days of her life.

13. She seeks wool and flax and works willingly with her hands.

14. She is like the merchants' ships; she brings her food from afar.

15. She rises while it is still night, gives meat to her household and a portion to her maidens.

16. She considers a field and buys it; with the fruit of her hands, she plants a vineyard.

17. She girds her loins with strength and strengthens her arms.

18. She perceives that her merchandise is good; her candle does not go out at night.

19. She puts her hands on the spindle, and her hands hold the distaff.

20. She stretches out her hand to the poor; yes, she reaches her hands out to the needy.

21. She is not afraid of the snow for her household, for all of her household are clothed with scarlet.

22. She makes herself coverings of tapestry; her clothing is silk and purple.

23. Her husband is known in the gates when he sits among the elders of the land.

24. She makes fine linen, sells it, and delivers girdles to the merchant.

25. Strength and honor are her clothing, and she shall rejoice in time to come.

26. She opens her mouth with wisdom, and in her tongue is the law of kindness.

27. She looks well to the ways of her household and eats not the bread of idleness.

28. Her children arise up and call her blessed; her husband also, and he praises her.

29. Many daughters have done virtuously, but you excel them all.

30. Favor is deceitful, and beauty is vain, but a woman that fears the LORD, she shall be praised.

31. Give her of the fruit of her hands and let her own works praise her in the gates.

We would love to hear from you
and hear your story.

Please email us at:
TheBookofProverbs333@gmail.com

FINAL THOUGHTS

A New Decision That Will
Change Your Life

Decide to read Proverbs daily and listen for the Word of God to speak to you personally. Try to memorize the verses, so the wisdom starts to direct your life at every turn. Tell someone about your decision. Then find a church that teaches the Bible and learn about the life of Jesus.

Where should you start reading to learn about Jesus?

The four Gospels—Matthew, Mark, Luke, and John—were written by four of Jesus' closest apostles. Each of these books recounts His life, the miracles He performed, and His instructions on how to live in the world as well as His death and His resurrection. Some say it's best to read the book of John first, followed by Matthew, Mark, and Luke. Wherever you decide to start reading, ask God to speak to you through His Word, and He will. Remember, prayer is us speaking to God, and the Bible is God speaking to us.

Blessings!
Dr. Gerry

A NEW DIRECTION FOR YOUR LIFE

Invest in wisdom daily; it will pay dividends forever. Imagine just reading a chapter a day and memorizing one salient sentence. Ten minutes of daily attention will get you unlimited benefits in wondrous ways. You will find yourself becoming ever wiser and, thus, healthier, happier, richer, and infinitely more influential. It will cost little and prosper you much. It is a shortcut to success, peace, and honor. It is a solid way to find wisdom. He who seeks wisdom will find it.

Invite a friend or two to join you on this sacred journey to ensure you'll be accountable, systematic, and regular in your readings. Read thirty-one chapters in one month. As you continue to do that, you will have a decided edge in every conversation, decision, dollar-earning capacity, and all relationships, and you'll be empowering those friends who take this journey with you.

Studying wisdom will shape your brain for higher discernment and inspire you to be the best person you can be. In the mind of God, character outperforms talent. As you grow, your character will be wonderfully transformed. You will have built-in decision-making software for a powerful life worth living.

The cost is not money, just simple attention to daily practice.

The book of Proverbs contains God's field-tested, compressed wisdom that has been proven worldwide for over 3,000 years. Treasure this book. Learn its lessons. Others will ask, "Who taught you to think like this?"

When you look back many years from now, you'll see a lifetime of advantages bestowed on you by reading through God's book of wisdom.

Mark Victor Hansen
59-Times Number One NYT's Bestseller
Co-Creator of the *Chicken Soup for the Soul* series, *ASK! The Bridge from Your Dreams to Your Destiny*, and the *One Minute Millionaire* series
Chairman of MarkVictorHansenlibrary.com

ACKNOWLEDGMENTS

I thank GOD for loving this world enough to create the original book of Proverbs and inspiring me to create an easy-to-read and easy-to-understand version to give away. I thank God for helping me write the stories at the beginning of each chapter.

My lovely wife, **Belinda Fox**, for all of her undeserved love and prayers and for taking time from her very busy real estate business and life in general to encourage me, read, and reread everything before I forwarded each chapter to my guide and mentor, Mark Victor Hansen, sweetly and unselfishly.

Mark Victor Hansen and **Crystal Dwyer Hansen** . . . Wow! Where do I even start? My friend, Mark, who was first and foremost a very talented motivational speaker, started changing my life over thirty years ago when I first heard him speak at a seminar I attended. He always was and still is a person who loves nothing more than reaching down and helping people up. Although we hadn't talked in over thirty years, when I sent him and Crystal signed copies of *The Book of Proverbs: God's Book of Wisdom*, he called me immediately, just like his true self, and began to encourage me. We talked just like old friends who had never skipped a beat. He told me how much he and Crystal loved the book and said, "The world needs more wisdom." He said they would like to partner with me to get *The book of Proverbs* out to the world. After a few conversations and formalities, the rest is history. Thank you, Mark and Crystal, my publisher at markvictorhansenlibrary.com, for being such a great source of encouragement, ideas, and enthusiasm from start to finish on this new project.

Additional thanks to Mark's co-editor and final manuscript reader, **William (Pila) Chiles**, an author, Fortune 500 speaker, and disabled elite recon Marine veteran, who said he loved working on this book to inspire more Proverbs readers.

My older sister, **Pam Fox Culbert**, for introducing me to the book of Proverbs at age sixteen. She told me about the very simple concept of there being thirty-one chapters, one for every day of the month. This simple concept changed my life forever. I am eternally grateful for her advice. This is what eventually led me to create an easy-to-read easy-to-understand version of Proverbs that did not in any way change the King James Version (KJV) but simply made it easy to read and easy to understand.

My parents, **Drs. Corbin** and **Faye Fox**, who taught me so many of life's principles throughout life that still guide me today. I'm also thankful that my father taught me by example to give books away and gave me a small booklet titled *Living Proverbs* at age twenty-one. This booklet, and his example, inspired me to give hundreds of them away until it was no longer in print, which, in turn, led to the creation of my first (successful) book and led to this new book with Mark and Crystal Hansen.

My brothers, sister, **Dr. Marlon K. Fox**, **Dr. Corbin C. Fox**, and **Dr. Lori D. Fox**. I am thankful for each of them, for keeping me as healthy as possible throughout the creation of these books.

Our absolutely incredible children and their spouses **Michael & Michelle Fox**, **Drew & Emily Fletcher**, and **Seth & Amy Parker** for their continual support, encouragement, love, and prayers. A special thank you to our son, **Michael Fox**, for his incredible leadership, wisdom and people skills in unselfishly running and managing our real estate company, The Fox Family Team of Carolina One Real Estate, to one of the top real estate producers in South Carolina.

All of our wonderful grandchildren for filling me with love and making me so thankful that I am a grandfather.

Stuart Hovermale, our very talented property manager and song-writing "lake son," who always seems to know when I need or needed encouragement, a mood change, or a good laugh. I am very thankful for his friendship and excellent management skills.

Tim & Sarah Jarriel, my brother-in-law and sister-in-law, who were initially the biggest supporters and encouragers of my first book by immediately buying one hundred signed copies to add to their Christmas gifts for all of the drivers, staff, and mechanics of their trucking company, Triangle J. Inc.

Karen Fox, my sister-in-law, nurse, who is always cracking the whip to make me follow doctor's orders.

All of my family and friends who continually encouraged and prayed for me as I was writing these chapter headings.

A very warm thank you to the thousands of people who encouraged me by accepting and buying copies of my original book, *The Book of Proverbs: God's Book of Wisdom,* which encouraged the production of this second book.

I am especially thankful to the thousands of people who saw the value in buying copies of the original book to give to those they care about.

Without the support, encouragement, and love from all these wonderful people, this book would have never been created.

My unending gratitude and love go out to all of you!

Many blessings!
Dr. Gerry

AUTHOR'S BIOGRAPHY

Dr. Gerry D. Fox
A Multi-talented Creator and Healer

Educated at Life University, he is a third generation Doctor of Chiropractic. His grandfather, father and mother were all Chiropractors. His two brothers, one sister, one brother-in-law and several other relatives totaling fourteen, have been Chiropractors. Dr. Fox interned in the largest Chiropractic practice in the world in San Francisco, California with Dr. Lloyd Latch and Dr. Ken So, where they helped 2000-2400 patients per week. He eventually set up a private practice in Charleston, SC. treating muscular skeletal, and nervous system disorders primarily through manual spinal adjustments to improve health.

After struggling through issues as a child, Gerry developed a deep faith in God which has guided and blessed him his entire life. His highest goal is to share God's wisdom with others that they too, may reap His greatest blessings.